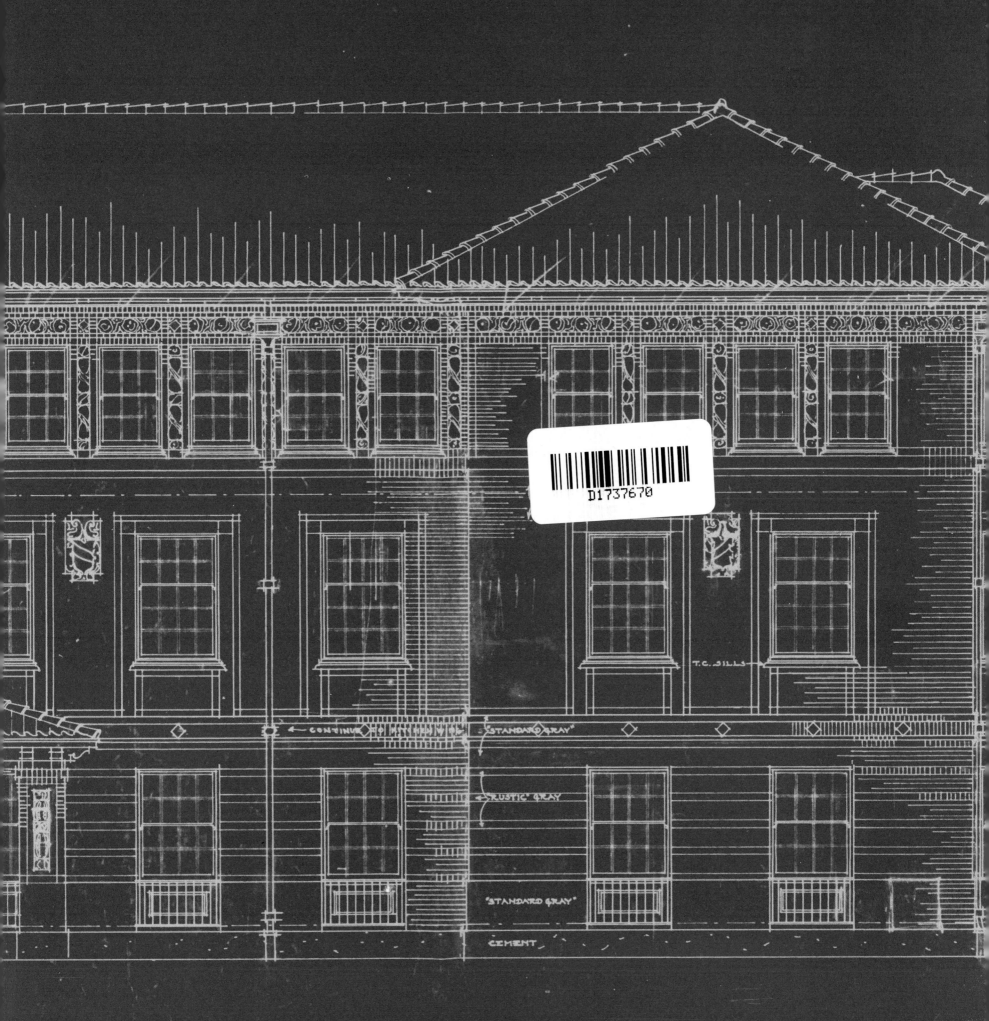

CONTINUE TO MATCH WINDOW "STANDARD GRAY"

"RUSTIC" GRAY

T.C. SILLS

"STANDARD GRAY"

CEMENT

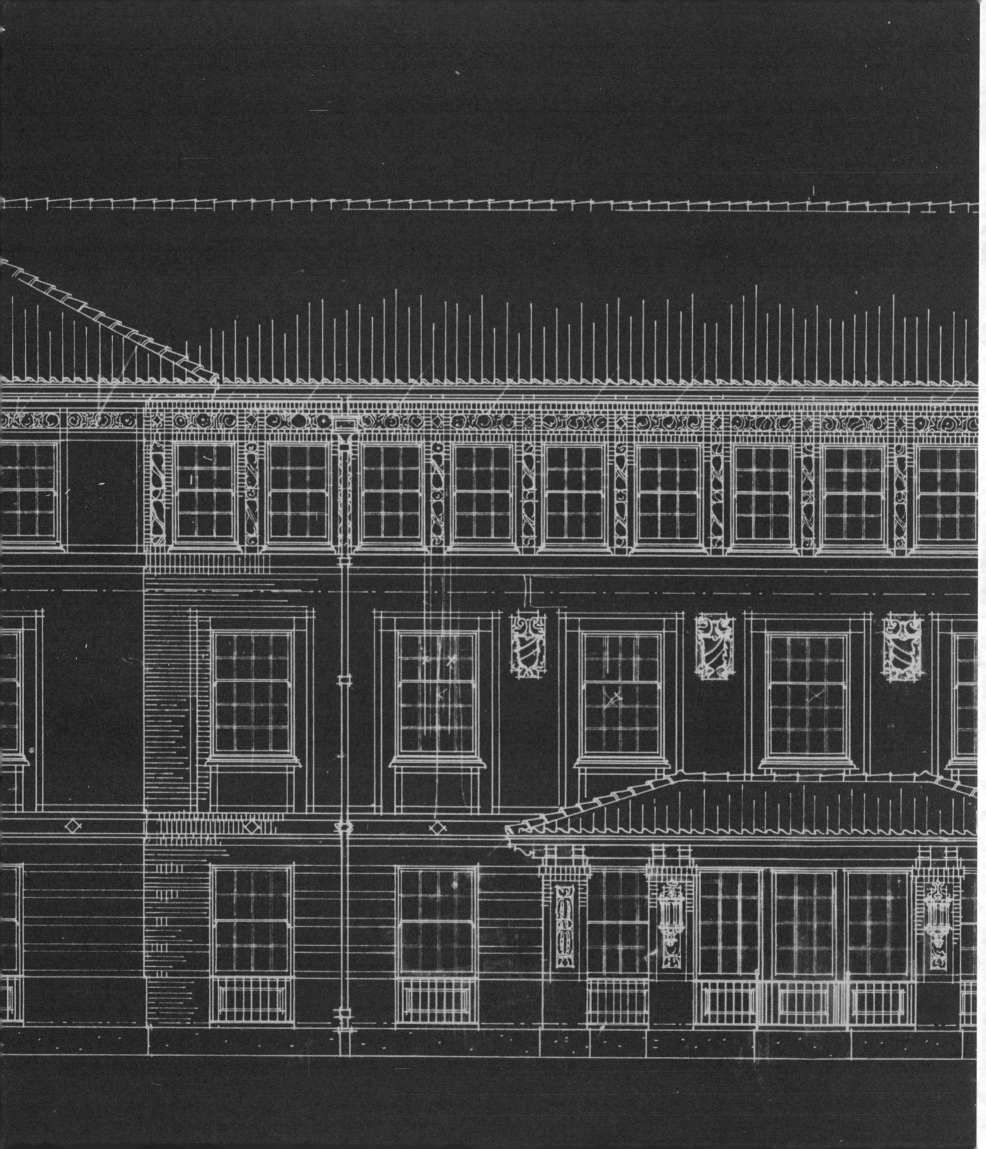

JULIA MORGAN

JULIA MORGAN
Architect of Beauty

Mark Anthony Wilson

Photography by Monica Lee
and Joel Puliatti

Gibbs Smith, Publisher
TO ENRICH AND INSPIRE HUMANKIND
Salt Lake City | Charleston | Santa Fe | Santa Barbara

This book is dedicated in loving memory to my father, Donald Drew Wilson (1925–2006), who taught me, "Do what you love—the money will follow."

First Edition
11 10 09 08 07   5 4 3 2 1

Published by
Gibbs Smith, Publisher
P.O. Box 667
Layton, Utah 84041

Orders: 1.800.835.4993
www.gibbs-smith.com

Designed by Linda Herman, Glyph Publishing Arts
Printed and bound in China

Library of Congress Cataloging-in-Publication Data

Wilson, Mark A.
 Julia Morgan : architect of beauty / Mark Wilson.—1st ed.
   p. cm.
 ISBN-13: 978-1-4236-0088-6
 ISBN-10: 1-4236-0088-6
 1. Morgan, Julia, 1872-1957. 2. Architects—United States—Biography. I. Title.

NA737.M68W55 2007
720.92—dc22
                    2007011260

Contents

Foreword
by Lynn Forney McMurray

She was oh so small lying there in her pale blue silk bed jacket. Little did I know what a mover and shaker she was. This lovely lady was an architect, an engineer, and my godmother.

My parents moved to Miami, Arizona, from their birthplaces. My father came from Philadelphia, Pennsylvania, and my mother came from Houghton, Michigan. Soon after they arrived in Miami they were sent to Downieville, California. Both were mining towns. My mother got very tired of a town without sidewalks. Northern Michigan had enough of them. She told my father that she was going to San Francisco to get a job and he could visit her on weekends. Needless to say, he followed along.

Mother was sent out by an employment agency to interview at Miss Julia Morgan's office. The agency told my mother not to be too disappointed if they did not hire her. They had already sent out over thirty people and none of them had been correct for the job. After the interview, she went to work for someone else. The agency called her and said, "They want you." And she was there for thirty-three years. She was even holding Miss Morgan's hand when she passed away. As Miss Morgan said at the end of her career, "I'm glad it was you who came to us."

My mother was hired to be Miss Morgan's private secretary. She, the office manager, Mr. LeFeaver, and Miss Morgan also oversaw the budget. My father had a building materials business, which he ran during the week. Weekends he would head to San Simeon. He was hired by Mr. Hearst, through Miss Morgan's office, to valuate Mr. Hearst's collections. They had to have someone they knew, because my father and the butler, Albert, who photographed the collection,

FACING: Angel detail, Hearst Memorial Gymnasium, UC Berkeley. ABOVE: Herman and Lilian Forney; valuator for W. R. Hearst and private secretary for Julia Morgan. Courtesy of Morgan Forney Collection.

went down into the vaults to work with priceless antiques, which were only shown to royalty. My father was a licensed and educated mining and civil engineer. He earned his degrees at Drexel and Lehigh in Pennsylvania and Michigan College of Mines in Michigan. He even oversaw the removal of a pier at San Simeon and accompanied artifacts to court for duty cases. He was packed to go to San Simeon when he had a brain hemorrhage and passed away. Mr. Hearst had died three years previously.

My parents had been married twenty-three years when they had me. They were forty-four years old. I was born and Miss Morgan came into my life as my godmother. She even went to the Episcopal service when I was christened and asked my mother to pick up a "blue frock" for me.

Miss Morgan had an inner ear problem with her mastoid gland. In 1932, she had an operation. The surgery paralyzed part of her face. The inner ear problem would cause dizzy spells. Once on a trip to visit Wyntoon, the Hearst family property at Mount Shasta, Miss Morgan fell through a flume, through a tree and rolled down a hill. She told Mr. Stolte, the contractor, and the workmen that if they breathed a word about this to anyone, they were fired as of right now! Mr. Stolte ran Wyntoon and Mr. Loorz ran San Simeon. Mr. Stolte couldn't get a letter off fast enough to Mr. Loorz. I've seen the letter in the San Luis Obispo Historical Society collection of Loorz papers. Miss Morgan would also fall forward into papers in front of her. Leaning on an elevator wall, someone thought she had been hitting the bottle. She had a miserable time with the problem. When they made the mistake in her operation, she was very embarrassed about the facial paralysis.

My mother encouraged her to keep going. My father commented in a letter to his mother that Miss Morgan rarely took meals with the group at San Simeon because of the operation. One good thing that did occur from the problem was that it brought new wealthy clients. Miss Morgan met Elsie Schilling, a member of the famous spice family. Elsie was in the hospital with a broken leg from skiing. Miss Morgan became known as Little Fish and Elsie as Big Fish. Many more clients were added to the growing list.

I taught twenty years of high school and twelve years of college. During the college years and after I retired from teaching, I was researching, giving tours and speeches on my godmother. One of my degrees was in speech. I had also donated five hundred Morgan drawings to UC Berkeley. I had my father's slide collection and Julia Morgan's office pictures, and I began visiting many of her buildings.

Miss Morgan was a true Victorian lady. She was a woman of class and distinction. She did not like publicity. In the beginning of her career, a magazine had written an article focusing on what a plain Jane she was. Here she wore beautiful hand tailored suits—blue or brown in color—always with a plain dark hat. Her blouses were specially designed for her in white or ecru. In college she might have been flamboyant in her wardrobe, but not in the working field. She was insulted by the article and said, "Let my buildings speak for themselves." Sometimes she wore a stylish cape, and was embarrassed when some children thought that meant she was a witch.

She was so private that she didn't like giving interviews for herself. She was very busy and very driven. She would always give an interview for Maybeck. She was contacted by the UC Berkeley Alumni Association. They wanted a picture of her. She didn't send one.

Miss Morgan lived in San Francisco. Her homes were on Divisadero near Pacific Heights. She had adapted two houses to suit her needs. One house had apartments upstairs and in the rear of the first story. These units she rented. The other house was one story and this was where she lived. I remember visiting her when I was a child. Her bed had been placed in the living room. My mother oversaw the nursing staff at the end of Miss Morgan's life. Mother was called to come to her home by the nurse when Miss Morgan was dying.

In the late 1920s, Miss Morgan designed the Berkeley Women's City Club. It is now called the Berkeley City Club, and was opened to men in the early 1960s. I thought every child had a club like this one. I took swimming lessons there, and I had my ballet recitals on stage in the ballroom. All of my friends took swimming there too. Even if the parents did not belong to the club, their children could take lessons. The club was Miss Morgan's little castle. She brought in antiques from Europe. She put different fireplaces in all of the main rooms. She did the same for Hearst at Wyntoon and at San Simeon. Mr. Hearst gave two gifts for the library. One was a Buddhist shrine and the other was a tapestry, I think. It was stolen years later. The night before the City Club was to open, Miss Morgan worked very late. She went to get a room at a local hotel, but they turned her down because she didn't have a suitcase. If you ever saw Miss M., she hardly looked like a lady of the night. Instead of calling her sister, who lived in Berkeley, she walked to the ferry to go back to San Francisco. She didn't want to bother anyone.

Miss Morgan worked until she was seventy-eight. She moved to a smaller office five years before she closed her practice. At the end there was just my mother and Miss Morgan. She wanted her staff to have jobs to support their families. Nobody realized she was doing less and less so she could gracefully close her business. When reading Miss Morgan's 1946 office diary, I found three short but sweet answers to job requests. The first was about a request to do a job in San Francisco. Someone wanted her to build a home like theirs nearby. She wrote, "Not." Next, there was a request for a home at Tahoe. She wrote, "Impossible." The third request was for a new home in San Francisco. She wrote, "Nope." When Miss Morgan left her office at the Merchants Exchange Building for the last time, my father asked her if she would like to close the door. She said "nope" and walked down the hall. She never looked back. She was getting old and she wanted to do a little traveling. She traveled on freighters, not cruise ships. After her last trip, she said they wouldn't take her again because they really didn't have a medical staff on board in case anything happened to her. Her last trip was with her sister, Emma, and Emma's daughter-in-law, Flora.

Miss Morgan was very kind and loving to her staff. In 1923, Mr. Thaddeus Joy, who was an architect and draftsman in her office, lost his home in the Berkeley fire. When the fire started, the family placed the baby up on the sidewalk, above the home. Someone thought she was abandoned and took her to the fire station. The family thought she had been kidnapped. They found her at the fire station. Miss Morgan arrived with clothing, soap, and towels for Thaddeus, his wife, and their five children. She later gave him a home in Berkeley, on Derby, for one dollar, the paper transfer cost. The Joys lived in that home for many years. Their son painted a mural on the dining room walls. I wonder if anyone ever discovered the mural.

Julia Morgan's drawing on a scrap of paper. Courtesy of Morgan Forney Collection.

Miss Morgan was never called anything but Miss Morgan, so I have a difficult time writing Julia or Morgan. As a child I referred to her as my Jul Morgan. I guess that was Hearst's code name for her. My mother couldn't figure how I learned the name. My answer is that children hear most everything. She called my mother "my friend." People thought she was a Quaker. The truth is she had a lisp and had a difficult time saying Lilian. She called my father my mother's "young man," although mother was only two weeks older than father. In the office diaries, she wrote notes to my mother or my mother left notes for her, identified with an F circled for Forney.

Miss Morgan would always get out paper and pencils for me when I visited. According to a cousin of mine, she did the same with her. She never offered me candy, although she lived on coffee and candy bars. Mother said she always had a candy bar in her pocket and kept her money in a small wrist purse. Miss Morgan always asked me what I was learning in school and what I enjoyed. When I drew garages, she thought they were marvelous. Little did she know that was the extent of my architectural talent.

Mother and Miss M. would leave little notes for each other. The last five years in the small office, Miss Morgan's office calendar diary was the receptacle for the notes. The notes extended to job requests too. Mother and father had purchased a Spanish-style home in Berkeley. Miss Morgan wanted to give them a house warming gift. She wanted to outfit both bedrooms in linens. She wrote to my mother on a tiny piece of paper what she was to purchase. She made two columns. Sheets—sheets, blankets—blankets, spread—spread. Mother found everything except a second spread. Miss Morgan drew an arrow to the second spread and duplicated the price of the first spread. Miss Morgan had a sense of humor. She wrote,

"Don't cheat me out of a spread." Miss Morgan did not care that mother had only found one spread. She insisted mother find two spreads. She was giving the gifts and she wanted all of the items in the package. The tiny slips of paper extended to office notes too. She would also draw on anything or any slip of paper. In her diaries she had sketched many projects or engineering requests. I gave a speech to EHDD, the architectural firm that designed the Monterey Bay Aquarium. The head partner told me Miss M. also drew right across someone's drawing to show the architect what they had to change. They had to start all over with their drawing.

She was polite and tactful. Mr. Gianinni, the Bank of America president and founder, went to San Simeon on a trip. Miss Morgan and he were standing in the courtyard in front of the main house, Casa Grande. Miss M. was standing in front of the two main doors leading into the house. She explained to Mr. Gianinni that one of the doors was original and the other was a copy. He pointed to the copy and said only an expert could tell which the original was. Miss Morgan agreed with him. She never told him he was pointing to the wrong door.

Miss Morgan never married. I am sure she would have been intimidating to the average male. She had more clients than most of her male counterparts. She was very dedicated to her family. She was a workaholic. Her few social encounters were mainly with her family. She had three brothers and a sister. She was very close to her mother and her sister. She also had a few couples she would visit for tea. She never really had time to have any romantic entanglements with anyone. She needed to focus on her work. She loved her work. She oversaw her brother, Avery, when he had a manic breakdown. This was the brother who accompanied Miss Morgan to Paris when she attended the Ecole. She also oversaw a home

Lilian Forney getting a haircut in Julia Morgan's office, c. 1920s. Courtesy of Morgan Forney Collection.

built for her mother on her sister's property in Berkeley. She designed the master bedroom in the house exactly like her mother's bedroom in her Oakland home so she would feel comfortable. On the back of the picture I have of her mother's home, she has written "ma's house."

Miss M. was on her way to San Simeon when Steve Zegar, her driver, had an accident. (Steve is the one for whom Miss M. supposedly built a dollhouse for his children in San Luis Obispo. Actually Ray Carlson, a draftsman in the office, designed and built the dollhouse.) The staff at San Simeon put Miss M. to bed in one of Marion Davies's nightgowns. Miss Davies was a much more buxom woman than Miss M. She didn't have her own room, as people thought. Miss Morgan hit the windshield in the accident and was out cold when the staff put her to bed. The staff went to check on her. She was still out, but the nightgown had been safety pinned up to the neck. She was modest.

After the 1906 earthquake, Miss Morgan was hired to bring the Fairmont Hotel back to life. She was hired because of her ability to work with cement and bricks. Many other architects were afraid of brick because so many buildings had collapsed. She redid the exterior and the interior. Later a newspaper reporter asked Miss M. how it was to design and repair the interior. Miss M. said, "I think you are mistaken. I worked on the entire project."

The office staff for Miss Morgan was very close. I have pictures of them sailing on San Francisco Bay. I also have a picture of them cutting each others' hair at lunch hour, when Miss M. wasn't there. I stopped to think that it was probably difficult for the working woman to get her hair cut, if they worked in the city. The staff also kept in touch forever. When I was born, they all sent baby cards. One of Thaddeus's daughters, Eleanor, was my mother's best friend. Miss Morgan was the one who watched over her own family, and she treated the staff the same way. They were her extended family.

Miss Morgan still has an existing family. Her elderly niece, Judith, Parmelee's daughter, passed away January 29, 2006, on her ninety-fourth birthday. I grew up with Miss Morgan's great-niece and great-nephew in Berkeley. They were Emma's grandchildren. I was a little older. Miss M. also has two great-great-nieces and two great-great-nephews. A new great-great-great-niece was born in 2005, and another great-great-great niece was born in August 2006.

Miss Morgan had planned to take a trip to Mexico. My father gave her a camera to record the trip. She wrote on the back of the pictures that she wasn't doing justice to the camera. The police tried to arrest her for taking pictures inside the churches. She did escape with a firm verbal warning. She was very embarrassed.

My father was at the Von Hachts, the lighting fixture expert, the night I was born. My father was trying to create a euphonious name for me with their help. Their daughter, who later became president of the Berkeley City Club, told me a special story. She said she and her brother took a trip to Wyntoon with Miss Morgan. They stood with Miss Morgan in a large fireplace. They looked up the chimney. Miss Morgan told them they could see the stars up there. The daughter said that they saw the stars. Or at least they think they saw the stars. They weren't quite sure. If Miss M. said they were there, they must have been!

Miss Morgan always brought me gifts from her trips. I still have a wooden doll from Sweden and an old mayo jar with a screw lid. The jar held coins and paper money from her trips. All of the old foreign money is still in the jar. When she closed the large office she gave me a baby angel, done by the sculptor Cassou, who did the figures in the Neptune pool at San Simeon. It is inscribed "A Miss Morgan" on the side. In 1943, Miss Morgan gave my mother a rocker that had belonged to Phoebe Hearst, Hearst's mother. It was given to mother when she was pregnant with me.

One can see the sense of humor Miss Morgan and Mr. Hearst had by looking at the tile designs in the kitchen at Hearst Castle. There are flowers surrounding several larger tiles. The larger tiles show Hearst with a noose around his neck and small castles. In Latin at the top of the tiles, it states that without work life is nothing. The tile is a Solon and Schemmel design. I grew up with the tile samples Miss Morgan used in her buildings. My dolls played on them. I thought every child had doll platforms like those. The tiles were Grueby from Boston, Batchelder from Pasadena, California Faience from Berkeley (Bragdon), and Solon and Schemmel from San Jose, who came on the grounds of San Simeon and did the tile work.

For several summers, I went to Asilomar in Pacific Grove for Episcopal church camp. This had been a YWCA. I knew my godmother had designed it, and I was totally in awe of the architecture. As I aged, I knew I had a very special godmother. I guess when I was younger, I was impressed too, but I didn't understand the full extent of her talent. When I was a child, I was with my mother in the dressing room of the Berkeley City Club pool. I was about two or three. I looked up at a plain gray shelf. Admiring the shelf, I asked my mother if my Jul Morgan had designed that shelf too. Miss Morgan and my mother later laughed at my choice for admiration.

Miss Morgan was practical and forgiving. She had a gorgeous Bokhara carpet delivered to the Merchants Exchange office when she first started her practice. When the workmen delivered the carpet, they cut a corner out of it where the file cabinet stood. When they moved to the smaller office, she told my mother to take the carpet home. She told mother to place her sofa over the cut-out and that nobody would be the wiser. It sat on our living room floor until all the color had transferred to the bottom of the rug. The pattern and the rug were wearing thin. It had the perfect pattern to play hopscotch. My mother wanted to be cremated in the rug. I forgot and I still have the rug. Incidentally, Miss Morgan was not cremated at Chapel of the Chimes. My mother is. Miss Morgan is in Mountain View Cemetery next door. She is in a family grave site.

We used to visit Miss Morgan's Monterey home. She added a second story to a Spanish-style home. The second story overlooked Monterey Bay. Guests would drive up Franklin to the top of the hill. They would park in front of a white hacienda. They would walk down a path with a gate, next to the white house. If you walked to the other end of the path you would find a massive stone garage. Miss Morgan's house was between the hacienda and the garage.

In the living room on the first floor was a large picture window overlooking a mass of scrub oak. If you crushed a leaf between your fingers, it smelled like sweet pepper. There was a Dutch door and a handsome fireplace. This room was fairly dark, both in furniture and color scheme. The breakfast nook and kitchen were light and cheerful. The colors were peach, yellow, and celadon. The second floor had a great room, then called a long sitting room. It had drafting tables lined up at windows that overlooked Monterey Bay. This room had Asian artwork. There was a

small bedroom on this floor and a massive bedroom with a canopy bed. I always wanted to sleep in this bed. One time we arrived and found the floors flooded. Mischievous kids had put hoses through the door and soaked the beautiful carpets. What a mess! We called the caretaker, Sachie Oka, who lived across the street. Together, we all mopped up the mess. I recently gave a speech at Asilomar. Sachie attended. She is in her late eighties. She remembered that incident. Also, she told me whenever Miss Morgan would visit her home, Sachie always had a hot meal waiting for her. Jesuits now live in the Spanish hideaway.

When Miss Morgan worked at San Simeon, she would get a roomette on the train. She would put a drawing board on her lap and work on her projects. In later years, she would leave San Simeon and go to her Monterey home. She did not keep a room at the castle.

Next door to the Monterey home was a Greek family with five children. The minute I arrived, I had to run over to see my friends. Later I read a passage in Miss Morgan's diary about one of the children, Dimitri. Miss Morgan wrote about a pudgy baby who changed into a gorgeous slim child overnight. Years later, a Greek family moved around the corner from my mother in Berkeley. The wife was a month older than I. The family in Monterey was her family. She loved reading the diary. She loved hearing the childhood stories. There was never a dull moment with all of the children near Miss Morgan's house. Miss M. was as mentioned, very Victorian and modest. I do not think she was shy in her business activities, but she was in her social life. A married couple for whom she designed a home in Carmel, near the Mission, attended UC Berkeley with Miss Morgan. This story was told by the younger daughter of this couple about her and her sister. When they were teenagers, Miss M. came to visit their parents. The older sister was sunbathing nude in the front yard, behind a hedge. Miss Morgan walked up the path and saw the teenager in the yard before she rang the bell. She was so horrified that she turned on her heels and walked to Asilomar. It was a very long hike!

Miss Morgan loved children. I think she would have loved to have one, if she weren't so work involved. She did place angels at several sights, as well as della Robbias. Mr. Maybeck loved them too and was a big influence. The mother and child or angel designs were in the Berkeley City Club and in Chapel of the Chimes. One was also in the original Wyntoon, designed by Maybeck.

Mr. Maybeck once told my father that one of his houses had burned. My father asked him what he was going to do. Mr. Maybeck said he was going to polish the embers. Maybeck taught Miss M. that there was never a job too large or too small. They shared several jobs. To name a few, the Lawson House, which was the first house Miss Morgan did, Wyntoon, and the Phoebe Apperson Hearst Memorial Gymnasium for Women at UC Berkeley, in which Maybeck assisted Miss Morgan. It was never finished. He was a mentor Miss M. respected. He encouraged her to go to school in Paris.

You knew you were loved by Miss Morgan if you still had your job. She didn't like people to ask for raises, and she preferred a clean-shaven employee, which is humorous considering Maybeck had a beard. In the front office were my mother, Mr. Lefeaver, the office manager, and Miss Morgan. In the back office were Thaddeus Joy, Ray Carlson, and anyone else who was doing architecture or drafting. The engineers like Steilberg and contractors came and went. It was a small office staff, considering all the jobs they completed. When Miss Morgan was an architect, it wasn't a litigious world. She once commented, "If you say a building is a Maybeck or Morgan look-a-like, it would be grounds for a suit." I'm sure she had no idea how large files would become to protect oneself from a lawsuit. Her medium jobs were only two pages long.

Miss Morgan loved the animals at San Simeon. She hired a client's son to design a two-story shingled giraffe house. They had a few giraffes perish. They realized that the animals were licking the salt off the small rocks in the shelter and accidentally swallowing them. They changed the material on the floor. They had an old gorilla. He was going crazy. Mr. Hearst suspected he might be cold, and suggested that they put a heater in the enclosure. The animal found his blanket and curled up in front of the heater. They never had another problem with the gorilla.

I spoke to a Glide family member in Davis about various buildings Miss M. did for their family. He directed me to a cousin who grew up in

Berkeley City Club ballerinas. To the left is Sydney Patterson Otto and at right is Lynn Forney McMurray. Courtesy of Sydney Patterson.

Berkeley. Mr. Elliott told me when their home was built it wasn't finished on time. They had to live in the attic and cook in the basement until the home was completed.

I've been in over four hundred of Miss Morgan's buildings and remodels. It doesn't matter whether we like them or not. The people who originally had her design their home loved them. She designed from the inside out. The second and third generations loved them too because they chose them for the qualities they liked; little things like windows in the closets, pantries, windows that open in (great for washing, but difficult for window treatments), and pairs of homes that have entries in the center driveway. Often relatives built across from one another and wanted to greet each other when they walked out the door. These designs make her work special to some people. A few homes have planter boxes with faucets in them, both upstairs and downstairs. She was an architect ahead of her time. She designed her houses for her clients. She considered what they wanted and then let them know if their ideas were possible. When she worked with Hearst she always said he could have been an architect in his own right.

Miss Morgan was a treasure. I was so fortunate that my parents found her and that she became my godmother. I hope I have shown a side of Miss Morgan you never knew. I am pleased my parents chose to relate the memories, or I wouldn't have them for you today.

—Lynn McMurray
Bethel Island, California
August 2006

Acknowledgments

First and foremost, this book would not have been possible without the research and editing assistance of Lynn McMurray. Her sharing of her mother's office records, her years of independent research, and her generous contribution of time in reading over my manuscript, as well as her sense of humor, made this project a much more pleasant task than it would otherwise have been. Second, the superb talents of my two photographers, Monica Lee and Joel Puliatti, were essential in bringing alive the work of Julia Morgan. Their skill, dedication, and professional commitment, often under trying circumstances, made it possible for everyone to enjoy the creative and beautiful images you see here.

Certain staff members at various research libraries and archives were extremely helpful in the process of obtaining primary sources for my text or images for the book: Anthony Bruce and Leslie Emmington at Berkeley Architectural Heritage Association, Carrie McDade and Miranda Hambro at UC Berkeley's College of Environmental Design, Dick Apple and his staff in the Media Center at Cal State East Bay, Bill Buetner at San Francisco Architectural Heritage, Karen Fiene at Mills College, Ken Kenyon at Cal Poly's Kennedy Library, Christina Rice of the Los Angeles Public Library, Peter Hanff at UC Berkeley's Bancroft Library, Allison Rodman at Chapel of the Chimes, Mary Breunig and Nancy Johnson at Berkeley City Club, Mary Gottschalk and June Lim in San Jose, Sue Lee at the Chinese Historical Society of America, Debra Dalzuffo of the Architecture Foundation of Santa Barbara, Ruth Hern at the YWCA Administration of Los Angeles County, Kathy Fries at the Petaluma Historical Museum, Remy Fisher of the Ojai Valley Museum, Nicki Mierzejewski at the Saratoga Federated Church, and Philip F. Meads Jr. at the First Baptist Church of Oakland.

The management and guides at both of the California state facilities at Asilomar and Hearst Castle went out of their way to assist me in my research at those sites, as well as both of my photographers in getting the best possible images: Hoyt Fields and Dan Heller at Hearst Castle; Patrick Sheridan, Connie Breakfield, and Al Hittle at Asilomar.

Thanks also to the owner and staff of Mangia Bene Restaurant in Martinez, California, for their patience and extra service while Lynn McMurray and I reviewed my manuscript at our favorite table. And a special note of thanks to Marjorie Ott, owner of the Olalaberry Inn in Cambria for her hospitality and generosity while hosting my photographers and me.

All the editors and staff at Gibbs Smith, Publisher, were both very friendly and dedicated in carrying out their various roles on this project, especially Carrie Westover, Jennifer Maughan, and Hollie Keith. And I am especially grateful to Gibbs Smith himself for his vision in initiating this book, and for his steadfast support and commitment to the project from start to finish.

I cannot say enough about the graciousness of the dozens of owners of Julia Morgan–designed residences, who invited me and my photographers to wander in and around their homes to document them for this book. I can only hope that seeing the beauty of their homes reflected in these pages will be an appropriate reward.

And finally, I want to thank my wife, Ann, for her support and patience during the entire project, and my daughter, Elena, for giving up playtime to come with me to see so many Julia Morgan buildings.

Hearst Castle, Doge's Suite, window detail, 1926.

Introduction

Julia Morgan's body of work spanned more than four decades, and her total output was greater than any other major American architect, including Frank Lloyd Wright.

She was a cultural revolutionary in a flowered hat. She was a "quiet feminist" who blazed a trail for women in a profession that had never allowed women to participate fully, until she came along. She was America's first truly independent woman architect.[1] Her name was Julia Morgan, and she was all of these things. But most of all, she was an artist—a creator of beauty who left an incomparable legacy of well over seven hundred buildings that delight the senses and inspire the mind.

I first heard of Julia Morgan when I was an undergraduate studying American history at UC Berkeley in the early 1970s. While walking around my south campus neighborhood one day thinking about a paper I had to write, I came upon an intriguing old building. Its walls were sheathed in redwood clapboards and weathered brown shingles, and it had a low-pitched roof topped by a wooden Celtic cross. The windows were more modern looking, with rows of tinted plateglass panes in "banded" style across the upper facade. The sign out front read "St. John's Presbyterian Church."

The building was open, so I wandered inside and was impressed at how spacious and graceful the interior was, with its warm wood paneling, open beamed ceiling, Mission-style chandeliers, and original carved pews. When I asked someone who was working there about its history, she told me that it had been designed in 1908 by a woman architect named Julia Morgan. She also informed me that I would not be able to enjoy this building much longer, since it was going to be demolished soon to make way for a new church.

Julia Morgan, Student I.D. Card, Ecole des Beaux-Arts, Paris, 1899. Courtesy of Special Collections, California Polytechnic State University (Cal Poly).

Today, that building houses the Julia Morgan Center for the Performing Arts, and is listed on the National Register of Historic Sites, as well as being an official Berkeley City Landmark. Dozens of Julia Morgan's buildings have been designated as national or local landmarks in cities throughout California, as well as in Hawaii and Utah. She also completed commissions in Arizona; Missouri; Washington, D.C.; Versailles, France; Jalisco, Mexico; Auckland, New Zealand; and Tokyo, Japan. (These buildings have either been demolished or not yet located, but Morgan's office records verify their construction).

Julia Morgan's body of work spanned more than four decades, and her total output was greater than any other major American architect, including Frank Lloyd Wright. Her best-known commission was Hearst Castle, that ostentatious compound which the multimillionaire publisher William Randolph Hearst asked her to design for him on property he owned along California's Central Coast.

In the half century since her death in 1957, Julia Morgan's reputation has grown steadily. When I first visited Hearst Castle at San Simeon in the summer of 1982, I was eager with anticipation at the prospect of finally seeing the most famous design from an architect whom I had written about in my master's thesis the year before. But the film that was shown to visitors then still misidentified Julia Morgan (who was shown standing next to William Randolph Hearst in one historic clip) as "Mr. Hearst's secretary." The docents knew this was incorrect, but they had to explain to most visitors who Julia Morgan was. Seventeen years later, when I gave a slide lecture on Julia Morgan's work in the Bay Area to the Hearst

ABOVE: St. John's Presbyterian Church, Berkeley, 1910. BELOW: Rosenburg Mansion, San Francisco, staircase detail, 1917.

Castle Docents' Association in that very same theater, the docents told me that the majority of their million-plus annual visitors, including foreign tourists, had heard about Julia Morgan before they began the tour.

One of the many reasons I wanted to write this book was to dispel the pernicious myth, repeated both in previous books and documentaries about Julia Morgan, that she destroyed most of her architectural plans and blueprints when she closed up her office in 1950. This misconception had its origins in the fact that she did indeed write to many of her former clients before she retired, telling them they could ask her to send them the plans for their buildings to insure that she didn't dispose of them. In reality, Morgan only destroyed a relative handful of her records, and none of her plans. Scores of her blueprints and other records were donated to the Architecture Library at California State University at San Luis Obispo (commonly known as "Cal Poly"). Hundreds of her blueprints and drawings ended up at the Environmental Design Library on the UC Berkeley campus. There is also an extensive collection of her drawings, letters, and architectural records at the Bancroft Library Manuscripts Division at UC Berkeley. In addition, I have personally examined thirty-five to forty partial or complete sets of original blueprints by Julia Morgan in homes she designed in Berkeley, Oakland, Piedmont, San Jose, and other Bay Area communities.

But the largest cache of Julia Morgan's architectural plans was in the possession of her goddaughter, Lynn Forney McMurray. Lynn has been a friend of mine for over twenty-five years, and she and I have collaborated on research to verify or disprove the authenticity of numerous houses alleged to be by Julia Morgan. Lynn's mother was Morgan's personal secretary for thirty years, and when Morgan retired, she gave the records for over six hundred of her commissions to her secretary to distribute to her clients.

Lynn inherited this treasure trove of historic documents after her mother died. She has donated over five hundred drawings and blueprints to the Environmental Design Library at UC Berkeley. She still has one hundred sets of original drawings, as well as the drafting record books from Morgan's office from 1919 until it closed, and the paper trail for all her commissions. So when my publisher suggested that we include an essay about Julia Morgan's personal life and office practices, I asked Lynn to do it, since she is uniquely qualified to do so.

When I was asked by my publisher to write down my vision for this book, I decided to take a different approach from any of the previously published books about Julia Morgan. The overall goal for this book is to inspire its readers to want to go out and explore Julia Morgan's unique legacy for themselves. Therefore, I decided to include only surviving structures by her in this volume, and not describe buildings of hers that have been demolished. I also chose to focus much of the text on some of her buildings that have been ignored or merely glossed over by other authors. For example, Morgan designed several fine residences in the charming town of Petaluma, in the North Bay Area, which are described and illustrated for the first time in this volume.

Another aspect of her career that I felt needed to be more carefully explored was the underlying design philosophy that guided a large portion of her work. Julia Morgan was, along with her mentor and lifelong friend Bernard Maybeck, one of the leading lights in a revolutionary design movement that has come to be known as the First Bay Tradition. In chapter two of this book, "Roots of a Revolution," I have explained in depth the origins of this movement, how and why it came to be conceived in the San Francisco Bay Area, and Julia Morgan's crucial role in it.

The physical, cultural, and historic settings in which Julia Morgan's buildings were created is another aspect of her work, which I have emphasized in this book. My ten years of experience as an art history instructor at several Bay Area colleges and universities has shown me that students are much more able to understand the significance of a work of art if they are provided with a clear and evocative description of its original setting and of its historical and cultural context.

Finally, I have ended this volume with an explanation of Julia Morgan's lasting and considerable influence on American architecture. While she never achieved the fame and public recognition during her career that architects such as Frank Lloyd Wright or Phillip Johnson did (indeed, she shunned such notoriety), Morgan's buildings nonetheless

LEFT: Asilomar, Visitor's Lodge, 1918. ABOVE: Hearst Castle, Casa Grande, South Tower, 1927.

have inspired numerous later architects to adapt her environmentally sensitive design philosophy to their own work. And her example of overcoming incredible obstacles to become America's first truly independent woman architect has motivated many young women to pursue a career in architecture, interior design, or city planning. I have had the rewarding experience on several occasions of being told by female art history students that they were influenced in part by my lectures on Julia Morgan to begin the serious studies that are required to enter one of these professions.

Julia Morgan's greatest legacy, which is the underlying inspiration for this book, lies in the elegance and sophistication of her work. Her legacy speaks clearly to anyone who takes the time to appreciate it: in the subtle beauty of her carefully crafted stairways; in the warm and intimate quality of her thoroughly livable interiors; in the pleasing refinement of every detail on her exteriors; and in the graceful strength of the structural elements of her largest buildings. She was a courageous pioneer in the forefront of women's professional advancement, and yet her greatest achievement lay in fulfilling a universal human need. Julia Morgan gave the world an abundance of that most valuable gift creative genius can bestow—beauty.

Sketch by Julia Morgan, Sainte Marie de Pontoise, France, 1897. Courtesy of CED, UC Berkeley.

CHAPTER I

Auspicious Beginnings

"They do not wish to encourage young ladies in their profession."
—Julia Morgan's instructor referring to the Ecole des Beaux Arts, Paris, 1898

The seeds of future greatness are almost always planted early in life, and Julia Morgan's childhood and youth certainly provided fertile ground for her natural talents to blossom. She was born in San Francisco on January 20, 1872. Julia was the second of five children: an older brother (Parmelee), a younger sister (Emma), and two younger brothers (Avery and Gardner). Her father, Charles, was a mining engineer from New England who had married into a wealthy family. Though Charles was an affable man who made friends easily, he did not have a strong business sense. Julia's maternal grandfather, Albert Parmelee, was a self-made millionaire who would often assist Julia's family financially during her childhood.[1]

But it was Julia's mother, Eliza, who had the greatest influence on her character. Eliza was a strong woman who ran the household in a firm and efficient manner, and who also maintained control over the family's budget. Meanwhile, Julia's father was constantly pursuing quixotic investment schemes that never paid off.[2] Julia was raised by a strong and dominant mother who provided her with a role model of an independent, capable, and efficient woman who could manage her own affairs. Julia's father was a friendly and well-liked man who was open-minded about people, which helped to instill in her the ability to relate comfortably and work well with people from all walks of life. Her parents encouraged both their daughters to believe they could accomplish anything they set their minds to, as evidenced by the fact that her sister, Emma, became a lawyer at a time when that was a very uncommon career choice for a woman.

When Julia was two years old, the family moved to Oakland, where they built a spacious residence in the latest Victorian style known as Stick-Eastlake.[3] It was two-and-a-half stories, and included servant's quarters. Like all of the Victorian styles popular at the time, Stick-Eastlake houses had lots of machine-cut ornaments made of wood and plaster, which were applied liberally to both the exterior and the interior. Their interiors were also dark and cluttered, with heavy curtains on the windows, statues in the corners, ornate furniture, and bric-a-brac placed on top of mantels and bookshelves.

Growing up in such an artificially ornamented home gave Julia a good basis to compare this type of aesthetic to the revolutionary design philosophy that would soon take root in California. Most of the late-Victorian styles of architecture stood in sharp contrast to the simpler and more nature-oriented homes that would be designed by many new Bay Area architects after 1895, including Julia Morgan. There was one Victorian-era school of architecture that rejected applied ornament and promoted a more natural style of design: the Arts and Crafts movement.

TOP: Julia Morgan, age seven, 1879. Courtesy of Special Collections, Cal Poly.
ABOVE: Morgan family residence, 14th and Brush streets, Oakland, c. 1870s, (demolished). Courtesy of Special Collections Cal Poly.

View of UC Berkeley campus, 1892, from "Blue and Gold" yearbook.

But this philosophy did not have an influence in the Bay Area until around 1890, just as Julia Morgan was beginning her college studies.

Two other factors in Julia Morgan's childhood were of importance in shaping her character, as well as her decision to become one of the world's first female architects. Her three brothers treated her as an equal, both by including her in their childhood games and in their later respect for her pursuit of a higher education, rather then getting married and settling down like most other young Victorian women. This gave Julia the confidence to expect and earn the respect of men when she decided to enter an all-male profession.

Equally important, both of Julia's parents were supportive of her educational and career goals, and they believed that women should be allowed to practice any honorable profession they were capable of. This nurturing environment gave her the courage to explore new paths in her academic and professional life and to persevere in the face of often daunting prejudice against a woman being successful in her chosen field.

Eliza Morgan took her children to live near her parents on the East Coast in the summer of 1878. They stayed there for a year, during which time Julia contracted scarlet fever. She was bedridden for several weeks, and when the illness finally lifted, it left her susceptible to painful ear infections for the rest of her life.[4] But she was never heard to complain about pain or discomfort during childhood, or later on in her professional career.

The family moved back to Oakland in 1879. During her stay in New York, Julia had met her older cousin, Lucy Thornton, and her architect husband, Pierre Le Brun. She became good friends with them, and would correspond with Pierre often over the next several years. Pierre worked for a successful architectural firm in New York City, and he gave Julia some valuable encouragement when she was deciding during her high school years whether to try to become an architect.[5]

After graduating from Oakland High School in 1890 with a very distinguished academic record, Julia Morgan entered the University of California at Berkeley. It was a young institution then, having only held classes on the campus since 1873. There were about one hundred female undergraduates at Berkeley by 1890, and two dozen other women also entered the university the same year she did.[6] But she was destined to become by far the most distinguished member of the class of 1894.

The UC Berkeley campus in the 1890s was a rustic tree-covered grassland, traversed by gently rolling streams and dotted with a handful of brick and wooden edifices. During the next decade, the trappings of a great modern university would arise, and Julia Morgan was to have a hand in creating them. The first step for the prim, quiet, determined young lady from Oakland was to take courses that would prepare her for a career in the previously all-male profession of architecture.

Julia studied math and science during her first two years at Berkeley. She was often the only female in her classes, since it was very uncommon for a woman to study such subjects at that time. When it came time to declare her major, Julia decided to enroll in the engineering program as preparation for her future profession. There were no schools of architecture in the western United States in those years, nor any classes yet in architectural design at UC Berkeley. So, always being practical, Julia chose to study the closest subject being offered at the university.

A handful of women had studied engineering at UC Berkeley before; indeed, the first female to earn a degree in engineering there was Elizabeth Bragg in 1876. But this course of study was still quite uncommon for California women in the 1890s, and Julia Morgan was the only female student in that program during her time at Berkeley.[7] While pursuing her studies in that department, she met an unorthodox instructor during her senior year who was to have a profound effect on her life and career.

Bernard Maybeck was an architect who was just beginning his Bay Area practice, and was hired to teach a course in "descriptive geometry" at UC Berkeley in 1894. This was in essence a class in architectural drafting by another name. But Maybeck also chose to offer the most promising engineering students an informal course in architectural design at his home in Berkeley. After Julia Morgan received her Bachelor of Science Degree in Engineering in the spring of 1894, she took this course from Maybeck, where she learned the theory of design in combination with practical application by working on additions to Maybeck's wooden shingled home. The group of students Julia studied with included some of the Bay Area's most distinguished future architects, including Arthur Brown Jr., John Bakewell, Edward Bennett, and Lewis Hobart.[8]

Maybeck espoused a radical new design philosophy (discussed in detail in chapter two). In essence, he believed that whenever possible, a building should appear to integrate with its environment, both in the way it fits into its site and through the use of natural materials. This was the antithesis of the Victorian-era concept, which held that buildings should stand out from their surroundings by displaying a plethora of machine-cut ornament to show off the owner's social status.

Julia Morgan found Maybeck's new philosophy to be a refreshing departure from the type of house she had grown up in, with its use of fashionable yet artificial decoration and lack of organic design. She would adopt these new architectural principles for much of her own work after she established an independent practice. But first there were major hurdles that had to be overcome before she could begin her career as a full-time architect, and Maybeck was quite happy to assist her in this process.

Bernard Maybeck, c. 1900. Courtesy of Berkeley Architectural Heritage (BAHA).

The first thing Maybeck did to help Julia proceed along her chosen career path was to hire her as an assistant in his budding architectural practice. She worked in his office for more than a year after her graduation, supervising the construction of some of Maybeck's earliest commissions in order to get hands-on experience in the field. One of the first projects she supervised was a residence in Berkeley designed for the noted UC geology professor Andrew Lawson, which was begun in the fall of 1894 and finished early in 1896.[9]

Maybeck also encouraged Julia to go to Paris to attend the prestigious Ecole des Beaux-Arts and earn a certificate in the architecture program there, as he had done. The Ecole des Beaux-Arts was the premier architectural design school in the world at that time, and most of America's famous and successful architects trained there during the late 1800s and early 1900s. Maybeck piqued Julia's interest in attending by telling her stories about the excitement of his own student days at the Beaux-Arts. But there was one major problem with this plan of action. The Beaux-Arts school had never accepted a woman into its architecture program, let alone granted a woman a certificate in architecture. But with the encouragement of Maybeck, as well as her mother and Pierre, Julia decided to go to Paris to see if she could gain entrance there.

In March of 1896, Julia Morgan left California, accompanied by her friend and classmate Jessica Peixotto. They made several stops on the East Coast to visit Julia's relatives in New England, cousin Lucy and Pierre in New York, and to look over several prestigious universities that Julia might attend if she did not gain acceptance into the Beaux-Arts. In May they sailed for France, and in June Julia and Jessica arrived in Paris. While her friend pursued graduate studies in economics, Julia began to study French and prepare for the entrance exam at the Beaux-Arts.

For a young intelligent woman interested in the arts, Paris in the 1890s was the most exciting place on earth. The works of Post Impressionist painters like Paul Gauguin, Georges Seurat, Mary Cassatt, and Paul Cézanne were being exhibited in avant-garde art galleries. The colorful Art Nouveau posters of Toulouse Lautrec were displayed on kiosks across the city. The innovative sculpture of Auguste Rodin was giving viewers a new way to perceive the human figure. The Eiffel Tower had been erected just a few years earlier for the Universal Exposition of 1889, and the city was beginning construction for another great exposition in 1900.

Julia had come to Paris with a set amount of money given to her by her parents for all her expenses during her first year there. She moved into a small apartment in the Latin Quarter—or student quarter—on the Left Bank, to save money. Even when her funds began to run out, she never asked her family for any extra money, but instead learned to live on a tight budget. This experience gave her a concrete understanding of how to handle money efficiently, which helped make her a successful businesswoman after she

TOP: Julia Morgan in 1896, shortly before leaving for Paris. Courtesy of Special Collections, Cal Poly. ABOVE: Sketch by Julia Morgan, interior of a Gothic church, c. 1896. Courtesy of College of Environmental Design (CED), UC Berkeley.

opened her own practice, and helped her to focus on keeping her projects within her clients' budgets.

The Beaux-Arts had a system of ateliers, or design studios, which all prospective students were expected to participate in before they took the very demanding entrance exam. The instructors in each atelier provided, for a fee, instruction in architectural theory and history, as well as practical experience in designing buildings as class projects. Julia joined the atelier of one of Maybeck's friends from his student days. All of the classes were taught entirely in French. Julia was the only female who attended the studio during her two years of working there.

When classes were not in session, Julia traveled all around France and western Europe, exploring the historic towns and villages and making drawings and sketches of some of the most interesting buildings she saw. Her drawings from these travels reveal a keen eye and a steady hand, and her attention to detail was a quality that would become a mainstay of her style of designing as an architect. Julia's enthusiasm for the beauty of the sights she was seeing in Europe is revealed in a letter she wrote to her cousin Lucy and Pierre soon after she arrived, in which she said, "I'm so glad I came. It wakes one up so wonderfully more than Boston."[10]

Finally, by October of 1897, Julia felt ready to take the entrance examination. On her first try she struggled with the math, since everything was in the metric system, which she had never used before coming to France. Julia placed a respectable forty-second out of the 376 applicants. But since the Ecole only accepted the top thirty, she had to try again. The second time she took the exam, in April of 1898, she placed well above thirtieth, but her marks were arbitrarily lowered by the examiners. When Julia asked the head of her atelier why this had happened, he replied, "It is because they do not wish to encourage young ladies in their profession."[11]

On her third try, in October of 1898, Julia placed thirteenth, and the examiners were too embarrassed to deny her entry again. So Julia Morgan was finally granted acceptance to the architecture program at the Ecole des Beaux-Arts at the age of twenty-six, the first woman to ever have achieved such an honor. The *San Francisco Examiner* ran a feature story a few days later that included the following headlines:

CALIFORNIA GIRL WINS HIGH HONOR

MISS JULIA MORGAN IN THE ECOLE DES BEAUX-ARTS

FIRST WOMAN WHO HAS ENTERED THE

ARCHITECTURE DEPARTMENT IS A GRADUATE OF BERKELEY

STOOD VERY NEAR THE HEAD OF THE LONG LINE OF APPLICANTS

Julia Morgan in front of Notre Dame Cathedral, Paris, c. 1898. Courtesy of Special Collections, Cal Poly.

The rules of the Beaux-Arts architecture program required that students enter design projects in a series of competitions to be judged by a panel, and awarded points toward the total that were needed to receive a certificate of graduation. No student over the age of thirty was allowed to enter these competitions, so Julia had to complete all her work in barely three years because her thirtieth birthday was in January of 1902. The usual time students took to complete such a rigorous course of study was five years, which was how long Bernard Maybeck had taken. But Julia was determined not to let anything stand in the way of her getting a certificate in architecture, so she plunged into her work with an unshakable sense of purpose, which was to be the approach she would take to every task she would face throughout her career.

During her studies in Paris, Julia attracted the attention of Mrs. Phoebe Apperson Hearst, the widow of the mining tycoon George Hearst and the mother of the famous publishing mogul William Randolph Hearst. Phoebe Hearst was one of the wealthiest women in America, and she had made it her mission to help make the new University of California at Berkeley one of the nation's greatest institutions of higher learning. To that end she frequently offered her assistance to some of the university's most promising students. Phoebe was probably familiar with Julia's architectural aspirations from the design contests she had entered while a student at UC Berkeley. Bernard Maybeck had told Mrs.

Hearst of Julia's determination in the face of staggering odds, so in 1899 Phoebe went to Paris and paid a visit to the struggling young woman to offer her financial assistance. At this point, Julia was sharing an apartment with her recently arrived brother Avery and supporting him financially, which only added to her burdens. (Years later, Avery developed a depression illness, and Julia took care of him the rest of his life).[12]

Julia's surprising response to Phoebe's offer revealed much about the qualities that would make her such a success in her chosen field: "If I honestly thought that more money freedom would make my work better," she replied by letter after Phoebe's visit, "I would be tempted to accept your offer. But I am sure it has not been the physical work which has been or will be hardest, for I am used to it and strong, but rather the months of striving against home sickness [sic] and the nervous strain of examinations." Though she declined Mrs. Hearst's offer, Julia thanked

TOP: Julia Morgan in her Paris apartment, 1899. Courtesy of Special Collections, Cal Poly. ABOVE: Student work by Julia Morgan, Ecole des Beaux-Arts, design for an archway, c. 1900. Courtesy of CED, UC Berkeley.

her for being so kind and helpful, and the two women struck up a friendship that would lead to several major architectural projects over the next twenty years.[13]

The style of architecture that was taught at the Beaux-Arts was an ornate form of neoclassic design. This style had developed in France during the later half of the nineteenth century, and was essentially Renaissance Revival rendered in modern materials. Paris was full of monuments in the Beaux-Arts style, the most famous of which was the Paris Opera House. All of Julia's design competitions were done in the Beaux-Arts style, and she received very high marks on every one of them. In January of 1902, she submitted her final student design, a plan for a theater in a palace. She was awarded first prize for this design, giving her enough points to earn her certificate just before her thirtieth birthday.

Before leaving France, Julia completed her first independent commission. It was a grand salon for a seventeenth-century house that had been purchased by an expatriate American (it was demolished in 1954) in the town of Fontainebleau.[14] Late in 1902, Julia returned at last to California, where she was eager to begin her new career. Back at her parents' home in Oakland, she set up her first office in their former carriage house. She soon hired several draftsmen and worked out of this cramped space for a year and a half. During this period, Julia was retained by the head of the new School of Architecture at UC Berkeley, John Galen Howard, to assist with the completion of two of the university's most important new monuments as part of a master plan inaugurated by Phoebe Hearst.

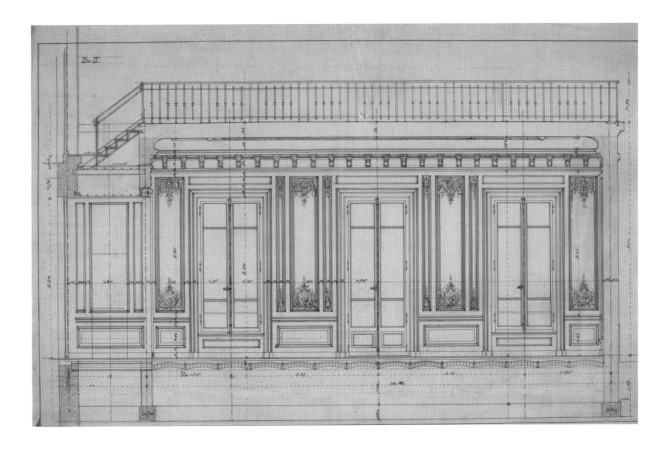

John Galen Howard was an accomplished architect from New York State who had also attended the Ecole des Beaux-Arts. He had been hired by the university to implement and refine a previously approved master plan for the new campus. Howard's revised plan envisioned a Beaux-Arts-style academic community with a unifying theme of white granite facades and red tile roofs. Morgan did some working drawings for Howard's office and supervised the construction of the first two structures begun under this master plan: the Hearst Memorial Mining Building (1902), dedicated by Phoebe Hearst to the memory of her late husband; and the Hearst Greek Theater (1903), which was patterned after the great outdoor amphitheater at Epidaurus in Ancient Greece. Both of these structures remain intact on the UC Berkeley campus, and they are among the most well-used and well-loved facilities by students at the university.

Julia Morgan might well have stayed as a "draftsman" in John Galen Howard's employ for many more years were it not for an incident that motivated her to move on. One day at a faculty event, Howard was waxing enthusiastic about the talents of one of his staff. He was speaking about Morgan but did not identify her until the end of his chatter, when he stated, "And the best thing about this person is, I pay her almost nothing, as it is a woman!"[15]

This comment got back to Julia Morgan the next day (perhaps it was Maybeck who told her, since he had no love for the pompous Howard).

As soon as she heard it, she began making preparations to start her own full-time practice. In February of 1904, she took the California state examination to be certified as a professional architect, and in March she received her official certification.[16] Julia Morgan at last opened her own office on Montgomery Street in San Francisco in the spring of 1904, making her the first woman in the United States to be a certified architect with a full-time independent practice.

TOP: Drawing for Salon of Fearing House, Versailles, France, 1902. Courtesy of CED, UC Berkeley. ABOVE: Hearst Mining Building, UC Berkeley campus, designed by John Galen Howard, assisted by Julia Morgan, 1902–7.

Sausalito Women's Club, interior, 1916–18.

CHAPTER 2

Roots of a Revolution

"In their freest work they fused historic elements into spontaneous expressions that belong to a high order of architecture in this country."

—Allen Temko, architecture critic, 1959

During the years that Julia Morgan spent studying to become an architect, a fresh new design philosophy was taking hold in the Bay Area. This movement was a reaction against the artificial ornament and ostentation of the Victorian era. It emphasized the use of natural materials and integrating buildings with their surroundings. The movement came to be known as the First Bay Tradition, and Julia Morgan would become one of its leading practitioners. In order to appreciate the revolutionary nature and impact of the First Bay Tradition, it is necessary to understand its roots and development.

The first stirrings of an aesthetic reaction against the high tide of Victorian excess occurred in England in the late 1860s. A new design philosophy known as the Arts and Crafts movement was begun under William Morris, an interior designer and furniture maker. He developed a system of design based on the use of handmade objects, which took their inspiration from nature rather than past styles, in order to achieve a simple beauty through harmony of line and rich colors. The movement Morris inspired grew by the end of the nineteenth century to include such prominent architects as Charles Voysey in England and Charles Rennie Macintosh in Scotland. Their residential designs emphasized the handiwork of traditional craftsmen and drew upon peasant culture in designing homes with simple, uncluttered interiors and built-ins made of natural materials.

Meanwhile, in the United States, many Americans began reacting against what they felt were foreign influences in their art and culture and turned instead to what they saw as more native values. These designers and their patrons began to look beyond the ornate Victorian styles imported from England. The Colonial American Arts and Crafts exhibits at the Philadelphia Centennial Exposition of 1876 were a catalyst for this movement. Thus, by the early 1880s, a number of wealthy East Coast families were employing the leading American architects of the day to design summer homes for them in various colonial modes. One of the more popular types they adapted were the seventeenth-century shingled saltboxes of medieval form, which survived throughout the New England countryside. Such homes served as an inspiration for young architects like Henry H. Richardson, who designed rambling wood-frame houses sheathed entirely in unpainted shingles during the 1880s and '90s.

These designs formed the basis for the East Coast Shingle style. These buildings often combined elements of traditional Japanese domestic architecture, which had also been exhibited at the Philadelphia Centennial. Low-angled rooflines and plain balconies from Japanese architecture were used on the exteriors, while elements taken from the English Arts and Crafts movement were applied to the interior décor to create a new and simpler type of domestic design.

By the time the designs of the Arts and Crafts movement and the Shingle style began appearing in West Coast publications in the late 1880s and early '90s, a rising young generation of architects and their patrons were ready to adopt this new aesthetic philosophy. No urban area in the United States was more receptive to these ideas than the San Francisco Bay Area. The hills of the East Bay were experiencing their first spurt of settlement, as people were attracted by the hospitable climate, cheap land, expanding university at Berkeley, and the sheer physical beauty of the natural environment. The conservation movement begun in the East Bay by John Muir, founder of the Sierra Club, had done much to raise the consciousness of Northern Californians to the need to preserve the quality of their special environment, even as it was being developed. Combined with this concern for natural beauty was a growing interest in historic preservation, which was first expressed by

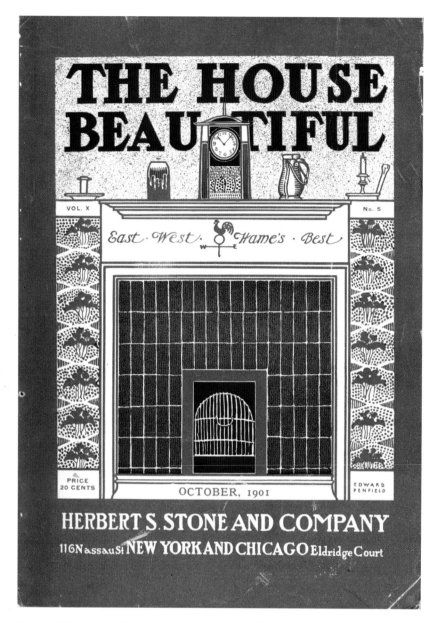

Cover of *House Beautiful* magazine, published in California, 1901. Courtesy of BAHA.

Both Maybeck and Morgan employed a specific set of design principles that were the guiding philosophy of the First Bay Tradition movement. These principles were first set forth in 1904 in a book titled *The Simple Home*, written by Bernard Maybeck's first client, Charles Keeler. In this book, for which Maybeck wrote the foreword, these guiding principles were defined and explained for the enlightened homebuilder.

There were four aspects that all First Bay Tradition structures had in common:

1. They utilized undisguised natural materials from the local environment, such as redwood, cedar, and oak, as well as brick and stone (or as Maybeck put it, they employed "an open use of natural materials, honestly stated").

2. They combined historic motifs, such as Gothic arches, and traditional craftsmanship with modern building materials and construction methods, such as reinforced concrete, asbestos siding, and plateglass windows.

3. They were carefully integrated with their surroundings, both through their use of site-sensitive designs and natural materials (so as to blend in with the hilly evergreen environment), and by bringing "the outdoors indoors," with such devices as large areas of glass, balconies, and decks to allow sunlight and breezes from outside to flow through the interiors.

4. Each building was a unique design unto itself, an original work of art that fulfilled the specific needs of the client and the community.

The Pulitzer Prize–winning architecture critic Allan Temko, in one of the first articles ever published on the importance of the First Bay Tradition group of architects, wrote in 1959, "They simply did not fall into the error of Le Corbusier of assuming that a machine aesthetic is in itself a guarantee of modernity. . . . They all used eclectic devices— Gothic tracery, Swiss balconies, Georgian doorways, Renaissance windows, Corinthian capitals. But in their freest work they fused historic elements into spontaneous expressions that belong to a high order of architecture in this country."[1]

A prime example of how Julia Morgan applied these aesthetic principles can be seen in the structures she designed known collectively as Old St. John's Presbyterian Church at 2640 College Avenue in Berkeley. This was perhaps Morgan's finest essay in the First Bay Tradition. Her work on this commission consisted of the following segments: the Fellowship Hall, or the meeting and recreational rooms, designed in 1908 with an early partner in her firm, Ira Wilson Hoover; the Sanctuary, or the main

a movement to preserve the old Spanish Missions and adobe homes that were in various states of disrepair throughout California.

These conditions combined around 1890 to create an atmosphere in the Bay Area that lead to an innovative and unique architectural movement that would come to be known at the First Bay Tradition. Bernard Maybeck was in the forefront of this cultural revolution. But his star pupil, Julia Morgan, was to play an equally important role as a leading light in this new movement. Morgan's range of designs included Period Revival mansions, Prairie-style homes influenced by Frank Lloyd Wright, modest brown-shingled bungalows, and monumental Beaux-Arts public buildings. But it is for the warm, intimate, and thoroughly livable qualities of her tastefully designed First Bay Tradition residences, churches, and cultural centers that she is most admired.

St. John's Presbyterian Church, Berkeley, sanctuary in c. 1910. Courtesy of BAHA.

worship area, designed by Morgan alone in 1910; and the Educational Wing, or Sunday School, also designed by Morgan alone in 1916.[2]

The exterior of these adjoining structures display all of the essential characteristics of First Bay Tradition design. First, the modest scale of the buildings integrates so well with the one- and two-story wood-shingled homes around it that at first glance the site appears to be a large, rambling Craftsman-style house rather than a church. Second, the rust-stained redwood clapboards along the facade, the exposed redwood roof beams, and the redwood shingles on the rear are all made of natural materials taken from the local environment. Third, the wood-carved Celtic cross above the main gable and the Gothic arched, tinted windows in the clerestory along the top of the Sanctuary walls are historic motifs, while

the banded plateglass windows above the front door in the Sanctuary and along the adjoining wings are modern features using modern materials.

The interior of Old St. John's Church employs the principles of First Bay Tradition architecture to produce an aesthetically pleasing space, particularly in the serene elegance of the Sanctuary. It was constructed entirely of exposed redwood. The ceiling is supported by open cross-strut beams, which create a strong sense of rhythm. The walls are paneled in deep, rich redwood. The chandeliers are done in a modified Mission Revival style. There is a wide, deep stage in front of the pews, which was perfect for worship services, as well as musical performances by a large choir. And the soft yellow tint of the clerestory windows casts a mellow glow over the interior during the daytime, which helped induce a state of quiet contemplation among the parishioners. No other building by an American architect more perfectly suited the needs of its clients.

FACING: Mills College, Oakland, Ethel Moore Memorial Hall, detail of fireplace, 1916.
ABOVE: St. John's Presbyterian Church, Berkeley, Celtic cross on front gable, 1910.
RIGHT: St. John's Presbyterian Church, Berkeley. Photo by Mark A. Wilson.

CHAPTER 3

Solid Foundations

"She was far more accomplished in the area of building technology than any of the men I have known"

—Walter Steilberg, architect and engineer, 1969

When Julia Morgan opened her own office in San Francisco in the spring of 1904, she already had completed or begun work on several important commissions that were to set the tone for the quality and diversity of her work throughout her career. Her first independent project in California came from her association with Phoebe Apperson Hearst. Mrs. Hearst had not forgotten her first positive impression of Julia after their meeting in Paris in 1899. The determination and sense of purpose Julia had demonstrated at that time convinced the wealthy philanthropist that this young woman would be the ideal architect to design some of her grandest projects.

Phoebe Hearst contacted Julia Morgan early in 1903, when she decided to build a large estate for her philanthropic activities and social events. She already owned a modest estate in Pleasanton, in the rural foothills of eastern Alameda County, about thirty miles from San Francisco Bay. The existing structure had been designed by A. C. Schweinfurth from 1895 to 1898. But this facility was too small for her needs, so Phoebe asked Julia to enlarge and remodel the existing hacienda, as well as add a boy's home, guest houses, two pools, tennis courts, a bowling alley, a banquet room, and a music room.[1]

The buildings Morgan designed for Mrs. Hearst were named the Hacienda del Pozo Verona, and were in a Spanish Colonial style that resembled eighteenth-century Spanish fortified villas in Santa Fe, New Mexico. The project was finally completed in 1910. But sadly, most of the complex burned down in an accidental fire in 1969. It has since been partially rebuilt as a country club, but none of Morgan's plan was reproduced.

Another major commission Julia received in 1903 was from Mills College, a private women's college located in a then-undeveloped part of the Oakland foothills. Between 1903 and 1909, Julia was asked to design several important structures for the college campus, including a bell tower, a library, a gymnasium, and an infirmary. (Morgan's designs for Mills College will be discussed in chapter six, under "Academic Achievements.") She had also designed a handful of modest residences in Berkeley and Oakland before she opened her San Francisco office.

From the beginning of her own practice until she closed her office in 1950, Julia Morgan ran her practice in a manner that assured her clients they were getting the services of a top-notch professional architect who was dedicated to fulfilling their needs. Her first office was located in the 400 block of Montgomery Street, in the heart of San Francisco's financial district. That office was totally demolished by the San Francisco earthquake of April 18, 1906.

Julia opened a new office in the summer of 1907, in one of San Francisco's early high-rises that had withstood the earthquake. The Merchants Exchange Building, at 465 California Street, was a fifteen-story skyscraper that had been designed in 1903 by the city's leading architect, Willis Polk. Julia Morgan was involved in the remodeling of the building's interior after the earthquake. Her work can still be found in the bronze eagles and Beaux-Arts lamps on the exterior. She also suggested hiring the renowned maritime painter William Coulter to paint a series of murals depicting ships on the walls of the great hall, or meeting room. The marble Ionic columns, coffered ceiling, and vaulted skylights were her design.[2]

Ms. Morgan moved her new office to the thirteenth floor of the Merchants Exchange Building, where she would keep it for the rest of her career. From mid-1906 to late 1908, Morgan had a junior partner named Ira Wilson Hoover, with whom she had worked in John Galen Howard's office.[3] After he left, she was the sole owner of her business

FACING: Chapel of the Chimes, Oakland, detail of stained glass, 1928.

Merchant's Exchange Building, San Francisco, Great Hall, building by Willis Polk, 1903, interior remodeled by Julia Morgan, c. 1906–7.

during the remaining forty-two years that her office was open. Her practice was not a very large one, consisting of between five and sixteen architects at any given time. There were several young women architects who worked in Morgan's office over the years, Alice Joy and Dorothy Wormser being two who stayed with her for many years. But most of her designers were men, which was not surprising, since relatively few women were earning degrees in architecture or engineering during these years.

Julia established an unrelenting work pattern for herself that was to be the hallmark of her career. She worked on numerous projects at the same time. During her forty-two years of active practice, Ms. Morgan designed nearly 750 structures, for an average of about eighteen buildings per year. Most impressive of all is the fact that she personally developed, drew the

overall design, supervised the construction, and oversaw the details for almost every one of these projects! She worked for eighteen hours a day during most of her professional life, getting by on four or five hours of sleep a night and the single vice of coffee to shore up her energy. Her tiny, 5' 2" ninety-pound frame housed a dynamo of strength and dedication.

Morgan related to the other designers in her office like a professor to graduate students in a studio-like atmosphere, a method she had acquired from her years of study at the Ecole des Beaux-Arts. She was an absolute perfectionist regarding her own work, and she expected no less from her staff. Her insistence on the highest quality in all aspects of the work done through her office made her legendary to those who worked with her. Yet she could also be highly flattering when she was pleased with their work. Marian Simpson was one of Morgan's favorite craftsmen, and she described Morgan's outstanding characteristics in an interview she gave for the UC Berkeley Bancroft Library.

"A tiny woman, gentle yet formidable. A rosy little face, innocent of cosmetics. Snowy white blouse with a tie, gray coat, and a skirt superbly tailored, uncompromisingly long. . . . Her manner was simple. Pleasant, yet rather reserved. Eyes very direct. A low, clear voice. I've seen strong men tremble when she said: 'No, it won't do.' But her smile could be radiant, her praise warm and generous. Once, delighted with some stained glass work I had done (for the Chapel of the Chimes Mortuary in Oakland), she beamed: 'Oh, it's bee-you-tee-ful!'"[4]

Such anecdotes from the craftspeople who worked with Julia Morgan illustrate one of her most outstanding qualities as an architect, which can be summed with this phrase: "Attention to detail." Not only did she carefully oversee every phase of the construction of all her projects, she also closely inspected the work of all her craftspeople, from fresco artists to tile workers, from cabinetmakers to sculptors. If Julia saw handiwork that she didn't think was up to her standards, she wouldn't hesitate to tell the worker to take it out and do it over. This reputation for absolute perfection of every detail made her both feared and admired by her crew, and greatly appreciated by her clients.

Julia was also fearless in carrying out her professional tasks. This fact is born out by the recollection of one of the young associate architects who worked for Morgan before venturing out on his own. Walter Steilberg went to see Morgan for a job in 1910 after San Francisco City Hall architect Arthur Brown recommended her office. At first, Steilberg was a bit uneasy about the idea of beginning his career by working for a woman, despite Brown's enthusiastic assessment of her as "one of the most able architects in San Francisco." But Steilberg's doubts about Julia's professional abilities were quickly dispelled one morning after he went to work for her.

"I went to the drafting room and there was a ladder going from the floor clear out the window to a scaffold. Now we were 13 stories above California Street, and the scaffold was just a group of two-by-twelves with some two-by-fours tacked to the edge and some chicken wire on the end. Here was Miss Morgan coming down this ladder, when she got down, she just stepped off and said, 'Oh, you must go up and see what I've discovered. They've blamed the cracking of the terra cotta on the earthquake. But it wasn't that at all. It's due to a fundamental error in engineering. They didn't design the building for deflection, and under the load, in the course of time, the terra cotta cracked. It wasn't the earthquake at all. You must go up and see.' Well, I was scared to death, but I couldn't tell her that. So I had to crawl up that ladder when my only impulse was to lie down on the planks and yell for help!"[5]

Merchant's Exchange Building, San Francisco, detail of stairway, c. 1907.

The key to Julia Morgan's success as an architect, and one of the qualities that set her apart from many of her male contemporaries, was that she conducted her practice with a completely client-oriented philosophy. Julia saw her role as the head of a team that included her staff and her clients. She would listen carefully to the ideas, wishes, and goals of her clients, getting to know them and their needs before beginning a design project for them. In her residential work, she took into account every relevant detail of her client's domestic lives when she designed a home for them.

A prime example of Morgan's client-centered approach is the Mediterranean-style residence she designed in 1911 for Walter Starr, at 216 Hampton Road in Piedmont. Mr. and Mrs. Starr had two young children, and they wanted their home to be a warm and welcoming family environment. Accordingly, Morgan arranged the children's bedrooms around the hallway on the second floor, near the top of the staircase. Then she placed a large angled bay window above the landing on the staircase and had the walls of the landing covered in warm redwood

Emanu-el Sisterhood Residence, San Francisco, detail of entryway, 1921–22.

Group portrait of Bay Area architects in Julia Morgan's office, 1928, with Julia Morgan in back, Bernard Maybeck near front (in white coat with beard), 1928.
Courtesy of CED, UC Berkeley.

paneling. Thus, when the children came downstairs for breakfast in the morning, they would be gently roused from their sleepiness by the soft, early light from the bay window, helping to create a positive state of mind.[6]

The team-like approach of Julia Morgan contrasted sharply with the ego-driven attitude of many other successful architects at that time. Frank Lloyd Wright, for example, was notorious for pressuring his clients to accept his vision for the design of the buildings they commissioned from him. The owners of the Buehler House in Orinda, California, recall that Mr. Wright literally badgered them into making changes from their original concept for their home before he would agree to accept the project.[7]

Morgan has sometimes been described as a "client's architect." But this phrase is too simplistic, since it implies that she would let the client determine the design for each of her buildings. Although Julia did listen

to her clients' ideas to determine how best to fulfill their needs, the final design decisions were almost always hers. Even when she was working for such a domineering personality as William Randolph Hearst while designing his compound at San Simeon, she often dissuaded him from carrying out some of his more impractical or expensive ideas, convincing him to accept her more reasonable (and usually more aesthetic) concepts instead.

There is some dispute about whether or not Julia was generous with the members of her staff. A number of published accounts have stated that she regularly gave bonuses to her employees at the end of each year. Lynn Forney McMurray recalls that Morgan would fire anyone who asked for a raise. However, as Lynn herself witnessed, Julia did give a series of bonuses to her staff during those years in which her office made a comfortable

Fairmont Hotel, San Francisco, c. 1910, shortly after Julia Morgan rebuilt it. Courtesy of Fairmont Hotel.

profit. She was also known to give gifts frequently to the children of her staff, such as books, new clothes, or souvenirs from her travels overseas.[8]

The 1906 earthquake had left numerous large buildings standing in a semi-ruined state in downtown San Francisco. Most of these structures had been gutted by the fire that followed the earthquake. Some of them were demolished immediately because they were unsafe. Many others stood empty while awaiting the decisions of their owners whether to restore the existing structure, or build a new one.

One of the most prominent buildings damaged by the fire was the Fairmont Hotel, a grandiose, high-rise luxury hotel at the top of fashionable Nob Hill, which was almost completed when the quake struck. The fire had left the building barely more than a shell, with only the outer walls still standing and serious structural damage to the framework. The owner of the Fairmont asked several architects if they thought the building could be saved, and they said no. Then he asked Julia Morgan if she would take on the job of restoring the hotel, and she readily agreed.

Morgan's solid training and previous experience in engineering served her well on this project. She spent several months inspecting the site for structural defects and then drawing up detailed plans for improvements in the staircases, skylights, rooms, and offices, as well as the grand ballroom and the bar. Once work on the building began, it proceeded at a surprisingly rapid pace.

One year after the earthquake, in April of 1907, the newly refurbished Fairmont Hotel opened its doors to the public with a gala reception and banquet, to which hundreds of the city's most prominent citizens were invited. Months later, when Julia was asked by an interviewer why she had decided to take on the task of restoring the Fairmont Hotel when other local architects had said it would have to be torn down and rebuilt, she replied, "No one asked me—they just said 'Fix it.'"[9]

The work Morgan did in restoring the quake-ravaged Fairmont Hotel in less than a year gave her a national reputation among architects and engineers and created a marked increase in her clientele. Where she received only ten commissions in the year before she began work on the Fairmont, Julia secured no less than thirty-five commissions in the year after its completion. These new projects came to her on the strength of her solid and well-earned reputation as a superb engineer, an innovative designer and architect, and a dedicated professional.

Fairmont Hotel, San Francisco, current view of lobby, as Julia Morgan rebuilt it, 1907. Courtesy of Fairmont Hotel.

ABOVE: Walter Starr House, Piedmont, view of staircase, 1911. RIGHT: Ming Kwong Girls' School, Mills College campus, Oakland, concrete entry arch, 1925. FACING: Berkeley Women's City Club, view of dining room showing reenforced concrete ceiling reflected in mirror, 1929.

Julia never engaged in self-promotion, nor did she ever seek public or professional accolades to build her practice. She shunned publicity throughout her career, and rarely granted any interviews. This desire to avoid the limelight was due in part to her reaction to an unpleasant encounter she had with a female reporter from the *San Francisco Call,* a major daily newspaper. When the restoration of the Fairmont lobby was nearly completed, the reporter asked Morgan to show her the work she had done. After looking over this magnificent space, the reporter mused, "How you must have reveled in this chance to squeeze dry the loveliest tubes in the whole world of color."

"I don't think you understand just what my work here has been," Julia replied tersely. "The decorative part was done by a New York firm. My work here has all been structural."[10]

This exchange illustrates another important reason why Morgan was so successful in gaining major commissions from new clients and retaining the admiration, loyalty, and repeat business of previous clients. She was one of the best structural engineers on the West Coast during her career. Her experience in working with reinforced concrete, which

began with the construction of the Mills College Bell Tower in 1903, was a valuable skill that relatively few architects had during those years. Walter Steilberg, who became one of the most trusted engineers in her office, was extremely impressed with her abilities as an engineer. Nearly sixty years after he had first come to work for Morgan, in an unpublished article about his experiences in her office, Steilberg recalled that "not only was she one of the most talented of West Coast architects, she was also far more accomplished in the area of building technology than any of the men I have known."[11]

The Hearst family, both Phoebe Hearst and her publisher son, William Randolph, were also greatly impressed by the work Julia had done in the restoration of the Fairmont. After that project was completed, Phoebe recommended Julia as the architect for a number of important commissions involving large-scale construction, including the impressive Asilomar Conference Center, a complex of two dozen structures near the ocean in Pacific Grove, California. And a few years later, William Randolph retained Morgan to design what would become her most famous project, the Hearst Castle compound at San Simeon.

CHAPTER 4

For the Betterment of Womankind

Above these arches are quotes from the Bible meant to inspire the young women who sought refuge here. One of these quotes reads "The Firmament Showeth His Handiwork."

—Oakland YWCA Building, 1915

The inscription on the cornerstone of the Oakland YWCA Building, which Julia Morgan designed in 1913, is an eloquent reminder of her commitment to working with women's groups throughout her career. It reads: "Dedicated to a Nobler Womanhood."

When Julia Morgan began her career, women still did not have the right to vote in federal elections, nor were there any female governors or members of congress.[1] A handful of women like her had blazed a trail in male-dominated professions, but in general, women were expected either to raise a family or to keep to such "women's work" as teaching and nursing. Yet wealthier women were creating organizations and associations of their own to assist other women in improving their lives. Such institutions as the Young Women's Christian Association, Women's Clubs, and the Emanu-el Sisterhood for Jewish Women, as well as orphanages and hospitals for children and tuberculosis patients, were being organized by influential women in cities across the nation during the early years of the twentieth century.

As one of the few female architects in America at that time, Julia Morgan was in a unique position to assist these women's organizations by designing aesthetic and efficient structures for them. Much of her female clientele came to her through her former housemates from her years as a member of the Kappa Alpha Theta sorority when she was a student at UC Berkeley during the 1890s. Morgan received numerous commissions to design Women's Clubs and YWCAs, as well as churches and hospitals, from several of these former sorority sisters.

One of Morgan's earliest commissions from this group was a new Berkeley chapter house for the Kappa Alpha Theta sorority, at 2723 Durant Avenue. It was first designed in 1908, and then remodeled by Morgan about 1930. Unfortunately, her design features were almost entirely lost in a 1950 remodel by architect Gardner Daily.[2]

FACING: YWCA, Oakland, atrium. ABOVE: Berkeley Women's City Club, front doorway.

The Young Women's Christian Association had been founded in 1858 in New York City by a group of prominent and progressive women who were determined to provide a safe and supportive living environment for young single women.[3] At the turn of the twentieth century, young women were moving from small towns to America's growing cities by the hundreds of thousands each year. They came seeking better employment and more social freedom than they could find at home. There was also a flood of immigrants coming to the United States at that time, an average of one million per year, and many of them were young women eager to make a better life for themselves.

ABOVE: YWCA, Oakland, main staircase. BELOW: YWCA, Oakland, 1913–15.

Many of these young working women ended up staying in boarding houses or sharing apartments in seedy and unsafe neighborhoods, since that was all they could afford. When their plight came to the attention of wealthy socialites through newspaper accounts of such living conditions, some of these influential women decided to form a nationwide chain of residential centers to help their less fortunate sisters. Their efforts were inspired by the success of the nationally renowned Hull House project in Chicago. Founded by Jane Addams in 1887, Hull House was one of the first institutions to provide women with a safe haven from crime or abuse, and to provide them with classes that would give them skills to improve their lives.

The YWCA opened branches in dozens of cities across the United States during the first three decades of the 1900s. These facilities not only provided a safe and pleasant place to live, but also offered recreational activities, as well as instruction in nutrition, typing, stenography, budget balancing, music and dance, and in English grammar, composition, and literature.[4]

The list of YWCA facilities that Julia Morgan designed in three western states is an impressive one. The California sites include: Oakland (1913), Berkeley (1922–23), San Jose (1915), San Diego (1916–19), Vallejo (1919), Pasadena (1921), two in Fresno (1922 and 1924), Sacramento (1930), Long Beach (1923), San Pedro (1918), Riverside (1929), Hollywood (1925), and three in San Francisco, including those in Japantown and Chinatown (1930), as well as the Asilomar Convention Center Complex in Pacific Grove (1913–28). Morgan also designed YWCA buildings in Salt Lake City, Utah (1919), Phoenix, Arizona (1923–24), and two in Honolulu, Hawaii (1925–27), as well as Tokyo, Japan (1926–27).[5]

The Asilomar Convention Center will be described in depth in chapter five. In May 2007, the YWCA sold the building to a private investor, who plans to lease it to a charter school company.

Downtown Oakland, California, is a treasure trove of early-twentieth-century American architectural styles. Elegant Beaux-Arts landmarks, such as the 1910 City Hall, compete for the visitor's attention with ornate Art Deco movie palaces, such as the 1931 Paramount Theater. Many of the Bay Area's greatest architects created their best public or commercial structures here.

At the northwest corner of 15th and Webster streets stands the five-story YWCA building, which was Julia Morgan's first design for the organization. It was opened in 1915, and has been serving the needs of urban women ever since. (In May 2007, the YWCA sold the building to a charter school company, and the future use of the facility is undetermined as of this writing.) The style of this building is Italian Renaissance Revival, and the facade evokes a fifteenth-century palazzo in Florence. The rounded arched windows, pilasters, projecting cornice line, balustraded balcony above the main entrance, terra cotta decorative details, and overall

symmetry of the exterior are all features of this style, masterfully rendered by Julia Morgan. But it is the interior of this superb building that really shows Julia's talent for creating public spaces that both inspire visitors with their beauty and invite them to stay.

Suspended above the entrance level is a magnificent two-story atrium, or "light court" as such features were often called in the early 1900s. The first story is bordered by rows of Renaissance arches, or arcades, creating an elegant cloister. Above these arches are quotes from the Bible meant to inspire the young women who sought refuge there. One of these quotes reads: "The Firmament Showeth His Handiwork."

The second level of this light court is lined with raised, recessed aisles, whose ceilings are supported by neoclassic columns and pilasters. Above these two stories, a splendid curved skylight spans the entire court, admitting a soft, warm glow through its translucent panes. On north and south sides of this light court are two superbly carved balustraded grand staircases, with curved banisters made of rich oak. These lead visitors from the first level up to the raised aisles on the second floor, where one can appreciate the perfect visual harmony of this space from an ideal vantage point.

Julia Morgan employed a broad range of architectural styles during her career, and this versatility is demonstrated in two other YWCA buildings she designed in Southern California. These two facilities, in Pasadena and Hollywood, were both rendered in the immensely popular Spanish Colonial Revival mode. Yet each of these structures offers a unique interpretation of that style with Beaux-Arts overtones, as only Julia Morgan could have produced.

After WWI, the city of Pasadena experienced a building boom as its population grew along with the rest of the Greater Los Angeles metro-

ABOVE: YWCA, Pasadena, wrought-iron grillwork. BELOW: YWCA, Pasadena, 1920–21.

politan area. The city's civic and business leaders decided to create an elegant new civic center that would include several fine public buildings and cultural facilities to be designed by prominent California architects. One of these structures was the YWCA. It was designed by Julia Morgan in 1920 and built in 1921 with the participation of the local architectural firm of Marston and van Pelt. The building is located at 78 North Marengo Avenue at Holly Street, next to Pasadena's City Hall. It was sold in 1996 to a private investor because the YWCA couldn't afford to carry out the necessary seismic upgrade. Though it is no longer being used for its original purpose, the building retains its historic architectural character.[6]

Julia Morgan's design for the Pasadena YWCA, as carried out by Marsten and van Pelt, has two adjoining sections fronting the street. The main section is three stories, with symmetrically placed arched windows and a doorway on the ground floor, and a wide iron grillwork balcony on

YWCA, Pasadena, wrought-iron balcony.

Factory and the focus of the hopes and ambitions of countless would-be actors and actresses. Of the thousands of young women who flocked to Hollywood every year in search of a future in the film industry, most could not afford a decent room to live in while they pursued their fantasies.

The Los Angeles chapter of the YWCA decided in 1925 to build a facility in the heart of Hollywood, to be called the Hollywood Studio Club. The project was carried out under the supervision of Mrs. Cecil B. de Mille, and the building was to be designed by Julia Morgan. It still stands intact at 1215 Lodi Place and Lexington Avenue.[7]

The Hollywood YWCA, which opened its doors in 1926, is a highly individual interpretation of the Spanish Colonial style. It has open-air loggias along both of its side wings, which allow the residents to enjoy al fresco seating. The Lodi Street side is two stories, with three Mission-style arches at the entrance and a tiled roof. The section behind that is a three-story residential wing. The entire structure has red clay–tiled hipped roofs, pastel plastered walls, and latticed windows. This facility has housed thousands of women seeking fame during its six decades as a YWCA, including a struggling young actress named Norma Jean Baker (later known as Marilyn Monroe). Today the building no longer functions as a YWCA because of stricter earthquake code requirements for residential sites. It is currently leased by the YWCA to the Job Corps Program of the U.S. Department of the Interior.[8]

San Francisco's Chinatown is the second largest in the United States (only New York City's Chinatown is bigger). Covering an area of over thirty square blocks flanking its main street, Grant Avenue, this lively and colorful community has thrived here since the earliest days of the California Gold Rush in the 1850s. By the early 1930s, an estimated forty thousand residents were crammed into its overcrowded streets and alleyways.[9]

The YWCA decided to build two of its most important facilities on the edge of San Francisco's famed Chinatown, to provide a recreational center for young women from the Chinese community as well as a refuge for other working women in the city who needed a clean and safe place to stay. Julia Morgan was hired to design both of these facilities. At 940 Powell Street, she conceived a seven-story, brick and tiled high-rise called "the Residence." Around the corner, at 965 Clay Street, Morgan designed the unique Chinese YWCA.

The Residence was designed in 1929, and opened in 1930. It was created as an elegant hotel for working-class women, with subsidized rates. The exterior presents a solid and imposing Renaissance Revival facade to the street, complete with tall, round-arched windows on the top and

the second floor. It has three-story wings at both ends of the building, with an open-air loggia across the top story of each wing. Both sections have such classic Spanish Colonial features as red clay–tiled roofs, low overhanging gables, and pastel plaster-covered walls, as well as intricate Moorish grillwork patterns over the round vents below the peaks of the gables (this was a signature motif of Morgan's, which can be found in many of her public buildings and larger residences in the Mediterranean mode).

Hollywood, to the surprise of most tourists and even of many Southern California residents, is not a city at all. It is merely a district within the incorporated city limits of Los Angeles. By the mid-1920s, however, Hollywood had already attained its current image as America's Dream

bottom floors, quoins lining the edges of the central section, and wide, overhanging eaves and a low-pitched central gable along the roof.

The interior includes features that were considered a luxury for working-class women at that time. Julia Morgan felt that these young women deserved the comfort of private dining rooms, and kitchenettes in their units, so they could have privacy or invite friends to dine with them at home. Her proposals were considered to be an unnecessary extravagance by the YWCA directors at first. But Morgan persisted, and her ideas were incorporated into the final design. Today, the Residence serves as low-income senior citizens' housing and retains most of Morgan's original features within its apartments.[10]

The Chinatown YWCA was built in 1930, down the hill from the Residence and adjacent to it. This community-based recreation center stands at the northern edge of Chinatown. Morgan's design for this facility reflects her understanding of traditional Chinese architecture. The exterior bears a strong resemblance to centuries-old masonry buildings in such historic Chinese cities as Guangzhou. The thick red brick walls are pierced by deeply recessed windows, and an arched entryway with decorative tiles above it. There are two massive octagonal towers projecting above the entrance, and a squared tower above the west wing. The roof is clad in handmade clay tiles, imported from China. The wall above a quiet courtyard in the rear of the complex incorporates authentic Chinese motifs, such as glazed tile geometric decorations lining a raised walkway and dragon-like patterns worked into open grillwork over the windows.

The original interior of the Chinatown YWCA was dominated by a bright, spacious gymnasium, where local women took organized exercise classes. There was also a very handsome library, as well as other educational and recreational facilities. The design for each of these rooms continued the traditional Chinese motifs on the exterior, and all of the decorative details were rendered with the finest craftsmanship available. Today, this exotic building houses the Chinese Historical Society of America Museum and Learning Center. The interior has been carefully remodeled to retain the aesthetic quality of Julia Morgan's original design. The museum currently includes all of the original Chinese-style furniture pieces that Julia Morgan designed for the lobby.

In the Marina district of San Francisco, on landfill that was created for the 1915 Panama Pacific Exposition, stands a majestic retirement home designed by Julia Morgan in 1924 and now known as the Heritage. Rising three stories above the corner of Laguna and Bay streets, the elegant Tudor Revival–style facade of the Heritage is made with red brick and lined with pink terra cotta around the windows and cornice.

At first glance, it might seem that this is an unreinforced masonry building, which would have been a very foolish method of construction

TOP: YWCA, Hollywood Studio Club, 1925–26. ABOVE: Hollywood Studio Club, detail, 1925–26.

THE FAMILY OF HAZEL Y. & PAUL H. LOUIE
GARDEN COURT
滄海雷葡瑞英夫婦及家人花園

in San Francisco after the 1906 earthquake (brick was not outlawed as a construction material in California until the State Uniform Building Code was enacted in 1933). But the building was actually constructed of reinforced concrete with brick facing, and this structure was carefully conceived by Morgan to withstand a major earthquake. Graphic proof of Julia's engineering skill was provided in October 1989, when this building was one of the few pre-1933 multistory edifices in the Marina district to escape any significant damage during the devastating Loma Prieta quake.

The Ladies Protection and Relief Society of San Francisco created the Heritage to fill a need for high-quality housing and nursing care for senior citizens. Morgan's original design for this facility had included a lovely garden centered around a fountain. Most of the garden area was lost when a poorly conceived addition was constructed in 1958. Yet the interior of the Heritage retains its original warm and inviting ambience. A series of gentle concrete arches between pleasingly proportioned pillars supports an open-beamed concrete ceiling. These concrete surfaces are painted to create a soft, pastel glow for all of the common areas. A Tudor stone-faced fireplace graces the living room, and several large Oriental carpets are placed on the polished, red-ochre tiled floors.

Morgan incorporated a library, a chapel, and a health-care section into her design for the Heritage. This facility now houses about one hundred elderly men and women in an attractive and dignified atmosphere. Anyone who has ever searched for managed care facilities for their own elderly relatives knows how important and unusual these qualities are today in senior citizens' centers.

A San Francisco Jewish women's group asked Julia Morgan to design a residential and recreational facility in another part of the Marina district, at Laguna and Page streets, in 1921. The Emanu-el Sisterhood Residence was opened in 1922, and it included a large gymnasium, several

assembly rooms, and classrooms, as well as living quarters for young working-class women. The four-story facade presents a U-shaped, symmetrical design on the Laguna Street side, with a raised courtyard across the second story. The windows on the first two stories have Italian Renaissance arches with fanlights, and the main entrance on Page Street forms a recessed portico with a classical Palladian archway.

The raised courtyard facing Laguna Street illustrates the subtle elegance typical of Morgan's public buildings, with its graceful glassed-in arcade supported by Corinthian columns bordering the street, and a carved stone fountain in the center (now removed). The entire exterior is faced in handsome red brick. In 1969, this building was purchased from the Emanu-el Sisterhood and converted into its present use as the Zen Center, happily without doing any major alterations to Morgan's original design. The direc-

FACING: Chinatown YWCA, San Francisco, view from interior to courtyard. TOP: Chinatown YWCA, San Francisco, 1930. ABOVE: The Residence, San Francisco, 1929–30.

The Heritage, San Francisco, 1924. FACING: Living room fireplace.
ABOVE: Exterior view. RIGHT: Living room.

ABOVE: Emanu-el Sisterhood Residence, San Francisco, 1921, entryway.
BELOW: Emanu-el Sisterhood Residence, San Francisco (now the Zen Center).

of the Honolulu YWCA combines elements from both Moorish Spain and Renaissance Italy within a refined, three-story neoclassic facade. The overall effect on visitors to the building is one of having entered an unexpected oasis of "rest and beauty" with a "distinctly tropical atmosphere," to quote an enthusiastic June 18, 1927, article in the *Honolulu Star Bulletin*. Indeed, here one could easily believe that they had wandered onto a set for a 1920s Hollywood film, or entered a fantastic foreign pavilion at a 1930s World's Fair.

The graceful exterior of the Honolulu YWCA is quite pleasing, yet it gives little hint of the exotic features inside. In true Beaux-Arts fashion, the Richards Street facade is symmetrical, with a projecting central section matched by extended wings at each end. These three sections are tied together visually with quoins lining their corners. The main entrance has a Georgian-style open pediment above Corinthian columns and pilasters. The front door is made of rich teakwood, beautifully decorated with carved flowers native to Hawaii. There is a lacy wrought-iron balcony below the third-floor windows of the entry section, and balustraded balconies run across the third-story windows of the two recessed wings on each side.

Walking through the interior of the Honolulu YWCA, the brilliance of Morgan's concept for this remarkable recreation center soon becomes clear. After passing through the spacious lobby, with a comfortable library and sitting room to the left, visitors discover a marvelous open-air, two-sided courtyard that evokes thoughts of the Alhambra Palace in Grenada, Spain. Running through the center of this double courtyard is an impressive two-story loggia, with Florentine arches on

tor of the Zen Center states that "The design of the building, with its quality of light in our large public areas, holds a stability and calm to support the lifestyle of our residents."

Hawaii has always conjured up images of an exotic, tropical paradise. Its capital and largest city, Honolulu, has been a sophisticated metropolitan hub for well over a century. In 1893, when control of the Sandwich Islands (as they were then called) was seized from native Queen Liliuokalani in a coup supported by U.S. Marines, Honolulu already was a thriving urban center. The Iolani Palace, completed in the 1880s in the center of the city, housed the Hawaiian royal family and their entourage in a style befitting many a European monarch.[11]

Across the street from Iolani Palace, at 1040 Richards Street, Julia Morgan designed, in 1926, one of her most enchanting and seductive public buildings. Her unique concept for the Metropolitan Headquarters

ABOVE: Honolulu YWCA, courtyard with pool. Photo by Alan Uba. BELOW: Honolulu YWCA, 1926–27. Photo by Alan Uba.

the first level and a covered walkway above.

To the right of the central loggia is a large swimming pool, and to the left of it is another spacious cloistered courtyard for dining alfresco. At the far end of the swimming pool is a Moorish-looking projecting balcony above a ground-floor arcade. This balcony has intricate wrought-iron grill-work and an overhanging roof clad in red clay tiles. Above the balcony is the third story of the recreational wing, which houses a kitchen, cafeteria, stage, game room, and a large gymnasium. Morgan's use of open galleries atop the loggia and along the balcony of the recreational wing allows visitors an unfettered view of the pool below. Tall, thin Hawaiian palm trees planted around the sides of the pool complete the image of a tropical paradise hidden away in the center of a great metropolis.

The Women's Club movement in the United States began on the East Coast in the late 1860s, as many American women decided to band together to promote the political and cultural interests of their gender. The very first Women's Club was the New England Women's Club, founded in Boston in 1868.[12] For the first fifty years of the Women's Club movement, it was focused on getting the right to vote for women in national and statewide elections. But these women also devoted much of their efforts to improving women's educational opportunities, as well as civic projects that would benefit women in their communities.

After American women achieved the right to vote in 1920, the emphasis of the Women's Club movement shifted to constructing centers where women could come to engage in recreation, as well as educational and civic activities. They also incorporated residential sections into these buildings, where women of all ages could stay for extended periods while they worked, studied, rebuilt their lives, or just enjoyed retirement.

Julia Morgan was commissioned to design a number of Women's Club buildings in California during the early decades of the twentieth century. These included a remodeling and auditorium for the New Twentieth Century Club in San Francisco (1914), as well as the Saratoga Foothill

FACING: Berkeley Women's City Club, entry hall. ABOVE: Berkeley Women's City Club, 1928–29. BELOW: Berkeley Women's City Club, exterior column detail.

Renaissance, a period when Late Gothic and Romanesque detailing were sometimes mixed with Renaissance neoclassical features in northern Italy. The front doorway has a massive Romanesque arch above it, supported by columns and pilasters with Romanesque leaf motifs. The archway itself is embellished with a Gothic trefoil tracery pattern. Above the archway is a Renaissance corbelled frieze, and the central tower is lined with Romanesque clasping buttresses.

The triple-lighted windows just to the right of the main entrance have Egyptian papyrus-leaf columns supporting Romanesque arches, while the rest of the double and triple-lighted windows on the first and second stories are framed by Renaissance arches and columns. The massive front door and all of the windows on the first two stories are made of Renaissance-style diamond-paned leaded glass.

Upon entering the lobby of the Berkeley City Club, visitors feel as

Berkeley Women's City Club (1929). Of all these centers, the Berkeley Women's Club is by far the largest and most impressive. Located at 2315 Durant Avenue, one block south of the University of California campus, the Berkeley Women's City Club decided to open its doors to men in 1962, when it changed its name to the Berkeley City Club. The building was placed on the National Register of Historic Places in 1977, and is also a designated state and city landmark.

Rising majestically above its neighbors like a massive Italian Renaissance Palazzo, the Berkeley City Club is one of the largest structures ever designed by Julia Morgan, after the Main Building at Hearst Castle. It is essentially a six-story, reinforced concrete castle, with a total of forty-seven resident rooms, as well as a seventy-five-foot-long indoor swimming pool, a very sizable auditorium, a spacious library and reading room, a raised terrace that doubles as an outdoor dance floor, two grand dining rooms, a beauty parlor, a large bar, a meeting room, sitting rooms, and an authentic Medieval-style cloister in the middle.

The Berkeley Women's City Club was incorporated in 1927. The club's board of directors was determined to have a female architect design their new building. On June 28, 1928, they named Julia Morgan as the architect for this project. The total construction budget was over $500,000, a sizeable sum for such a facility at that time. Morgan's plans were completed in June of 1929, and groundbreaking took place on December 17, 1929. The project was completed in the remarkably short span of eleven months, in time for the members to have an open house on November 20, 1930.[13]

The exterior of the Berkeley City Club displays a wonderfully rich assortment of architectural motifs, which complement each other to create an aesthetic harmony. The overall style of the building is Early Italian

LEFT: Berkeley Women's City Club, library fireplace. BELOW: Berkeley Women's City Club, interior view of cloister. FACING: Berkeley Women's City Club, library.

though they've been transported back in time to early fifteenth-century Italy. Gothic groined vaulting supports the ceilings, from which hang ornate wrought-iron chandeliers illuminated by "electrified" candles. A grand staircase rises along the far wall of the lobby, with strange bear-like creatures holding shields guarding the landings, and Gothic quatrefoil tracery decorating the railings.

To the left is the doorway to the first-floor dining room, with a baronial fireplace and high ceilings spanned by concrete beams cleverly disguised to look like carved wood. To the right is a wide hallway and sitting area, with lovely wrought-iron sconces gracing the walls. The hallway leads to a small reading room at the end. This was originally the men's lounge and is currently the Julia Morgan History Center. On the right, just before you enter this room, is the entrance to the swimming pool.

Straight ahead, past the grand staircase, is one of the few authentic medieval-style cloisters in California (it only lacks a fourth covered walkway, along the rear wall). Romanesque arches and columns frame this open-air, four-sided courtyard. Between the columns there are large diamond-paned windows and doors that look out onto a lushly landscaped patio. Above the arches are Gothic octofoil windows, with tracery made from molded concrete that looks like carved stone.

On the second floor is the upstairs dining hall. This magnificent room has the ambience of a great banqueting hall in a Renaissance palace. The ceilings are supported by massive beams made of concrete disguised as hand-hewn wooden timbers. The elegant fireplace has a Gothic octofoil pattern surrounding the firebox, and a baroque gilt mirror designed by Julia Morgan above the mantel. The floor-to-ceiling windows double as doors leading out onto a wide balcony, and have diamond-paned, leaded latticing. The ceiling has large wrought-iron chandeliers hanging from the central beam.

Straight ahead from the top of the staircase is the spacious library, with its wide triple-lighted windows, "beveled beam" concrete ceiling, and an immense fireplace with three beautifully carved bas-relief panels gracing the overmantel. The doors on the right side of the library open onto a large terrace that is sometimes used as an open-air dance floor, and is actually the roof of the pool below. From here, there is a wonderful view of the cloister.

At the far end of the terrace is a doorway leading into a spacious auditorium, which can seat three hundred people. It has a high-beamed ceiling (this one has actual redwood beams), a large stage, and hardwood floors. Behind the auditorium is a handsome bar with a unique coffered ceiling decorated with hand-painted heraldic designs (the bar didn't serve alcohol

FACING: Berkeley Women's City Club, bas-relief panel of "The Three Graces," north courtyard. ABOVE: Sausalito Women's Club, sign overlooking the Bay.

until Prohibition was repealed in 1933). To the left of the bar is a large, formal ladies powder room, with a wide sitting area in front of it for gentlemen to wait for their lady friends. Men were only allowed to join their wives or women friends for special events until the Berkeley Women's City Club admitted male members in 1962.

The upper four floors are taken up with private rooms for the residents. Throughout the Berkeley City Club, there are carved figurines, della Robbias, mirrors, sculptures, bas-relief panels, and prints that were selected or commissioned by Julia Morgan herself, as well as several of her original color drawings, sketches, and studies of the exterior and details of this incredible building.

Two other Women's Club buildings designed by Julia Morgan have

ABOVE: Sausalito Women's Club (now Sausalito Woman's Club), 1916–18.
BELOW: Saratoga Foothill Women's Club, 1915, entrance with built-in benches.
FACING: Sausalito Women's Club, detail of staircase.

survived largely intact: the Saratoga Foothill Women's Club, and the Sausalito Women's Club. Saratoga is a wealthy, woodsy, secluded community on the peninsula, about twenty miles south of San Francisco. A Women's Club was organized there in 1907, and by 1915, its directors decided they needed to construct a permanent building to house their activities. They commissioned Julia Morgan to design their facility and, after reviewing four possible plans Julia submitted to them, they chose one in the Arts and Crafts mode.[14]

The Saratoga Foothill Women's Club integrates with its site brilliantly, and is a superb example of First Bay Tradition architecture. The exterior is clad in redwood and there are wooden pergolas extending into the gardens behind it. The building nestles comfortably into its gentle upslope lot and the low-gabled roofline complements the natural contours of its setting.

The interior integrates the natural beauty of the outdoors through the use of a wall of floor-to-ceiling windows on two sides of the building. There is also a large porthole window in the main gable to admit more light, and built-in wooden benches flanking the front door invite visitors to stay awhile. Morgan's design included a movie projection booth, a large assembly room with a stage, and a kitchen. This well-used building

still serves all of the same functions for which Julia planned it.

Sausalito is an upscale suburb of San Francisco in Marin County that clings to the hills above San Francisco Bay. The views of the bay and the San Francisco skyline from here are breathtaking. In 1916, the Sausalito Women's Club hired Julia Morgan to design their clubhouse on a steep hillside overlooking the bay. Her building for them, which was dedicated in 1918, is another fine example of the First Bay Tradition.

The building is constructed of redwood, with floor-to-ceiling windows along two sides to provide unobstructed views of the bay below. The facade incorporates several balconies to further enhance the ability of its occupants to enjoy the beauty of the natural setting, and the boardroom on the second story has panoramic views from all four sides. The exterior is sheathed in redwood shingles, which integrate well with the surroundings.

In addition to YWCAs and Women's Clubs, Julia Morgan also designed several tuberculosis hospitals for women in cities throughout California, as well as two pediatric nursing homes for children with terminal diseases. Among the women's hospitals, the one in Oakland was the largest and most important commission.

The King's Daughters Home stretches along the entire east side of the 3900 block of Broadway, two miles south of downtown Oakland. The original complex, designed by Julia Morgan between 1908 and 1912, consisted of five three-story Mediterranean-style buildings sheathed in yellow brick and roofed with red tiles. The main building facing Broadway remains intact, and it gracefully commands its upslope lot. The original entry pavilion for pedestrians remains at the south end, and an elegantly arched, Art Nouveau—style wrought-iron gateway still spans the drive-

TOP: YWCA Hospitality Center, 437 W. 9th Street, San Pedro, California, 1918, view from 1921. Courtesy of San Pedro YWCA. ABOVE: Salt Lake City, Utah, YWCA, 322 Broadway, 1919–20. Courtesy of Salt Lake City YWCA (tall section on the right was added by another architect in 1954).

way at the north end (this gateway was dedicated to Julia's brother Sam, who was killed in 1913 while riding on an Oakland fire truck).[15]

The King's Daughters served as a hospital for severely ill female tuberculosis patients until the early 1980s. At that time, it was sold to the Kaiser Health Plan, which demolished the buildings in the rear of the complex for parking. Today the main building serves as a behavioral medicine and psychiatry facility for the Kaiser Health Plan, and the exterior retains all of its decorative terra cotta Renaissance-style details.

Near the western fringes of Santa Barbara, at 300 North San Antonio Road, Julia Morgan designed a children's tuberculosis hospital in 1918. It was commissioned by Santa Barbara County, and opened its doors in 1919. The style of this distinctive structure is a unique hybrid of Mediterranean and Viennese Secessionist. The two-story facade has a loosely Spanish Colonial feel, with thick white stucco walls and a red clay–tile roof. But the entry pavilion has a series of tapering columns that evoke the extreme geometry of the Art Nouveau in Vienna, as do the two tapered concrete lampposts flanking the entryway. This building is still used by the county as a health-care facility, and is now known as the San Antonio Building.

ABOVE: Santa Barbara County Children's Tuberculosis Hospital (now San Antonio Building), Santa Barbara, 1918–19. Photo by Mark A. Wilson. BELOW: King's Daughters Home, Oakland, 1908–12, west elevation. Courtesy of CED, UC Berkeley.

CHAPTER 5

To Refresh the Soul

"Everyone needs beauty as well as bread, places to pray in and play in, where nature may heal and give strength to body and soul alike."

—John Muir, 1912

There are very few places in North America that equal the spirit-nurturing, natural beauty of the Monterey Peninsula. Jutting sharply into the Pacific Ocean about 120 miles south of San Francisco, it shelters Monterey Bay, one of the most serenely pleasant spots on the West Coast. Crowds of tourists come here throughout the year to catch a glimpse of the sea otters playing on the rocks, or stroll along the sandy beaches and smell the salt air.

Among all of the natural attractions on the Monterey Peninsula, by far the most tranquil and refreshing location is the State Beach and Conference Grounds at Asilomar.

Covering 107 acres along the coastline just west of the charming Victorian town of Pacific Grove, Asilomar means "refuge by the sea" in Spanish. A conference center was founded on the original thirty-acre site in 1913. Here, between 1913 and 1928, Julia Morgan designed sixteen structures, twelve of which have been maintained in their original setting. These buildings now comprise the largest collection of Julia Morgan's architecture in one location. They were placed on the National Register of Historic Places in 1987.[1]

The history of Asilomar began in 1912, when Phoebe Hearst convinced the YWCA at their annual leadership conference to construct a permanent conference center on the Northern California Coast. Mrs. Hearst then contacted the Pacific Improvement Company in Monterey, and persuaded them to donate a vacant thirty-acre site near Pacific Grove to the YWCA for this purpose. The following year, Julia Morgan, who had been hired by the YWCA to be the sole architect for the new conference center, finished her work on the first three buildings, and Asilomar opened in the summer of 1913.[2]

In designing the structures for Asilomar, Julia Morgan applied the principles of the First Bay Tradition, which required that all the buildings integrate aesthetically with their natural environment. This is a place that invites one to linger, listening for hours to the peaceful rhythm of the ocean waves as they roll slowly onto shore, or take a leisurely walk beneath the coast live oaks and tall Monterey pines that rise so majestically above the chaparral-covered dunes. In planning buildings that were appropriate for such a site, Julia was guided by a concept of nature that had been summed up in a 1912 quote by the great conservationist John Muir: "Everyone needs beauty as well as bread, places to play in and pray in, where nature may heal and give strength to body and soul alike."[3]

FACING: Asilomar, Pacific Grove, Pirate's Den, 1923. ABOVE: Asilomar, Pacific Grove, view of grounds with ocean.

ABOVE: Asilomar, Pacific Grove, Visitor's Lodge, 1917–18. BELOW: Asilomar, Pacific Grove, stone entrance pillar, 1913.

Morgan's general plan for Asilomar utilized a simple yet brilliant unifying theme. The exteriors of the buildings would be relatively plain and unadorned, so as to not distract guests from the natural beauty of their surroundings, and they would all incorporate local natural materials, such as granite boulders, Carmel fieldstone, cedar shingles, and redwood beams and posts. The interiors, however, would exhibit an impressive display of the finest craftsmanship and Art and Crafts–style detailing, and would provide visitors an aesthetic and inspiring ambience in which to think, pray, read, eat, or simply relax.

The first building to be completed by Morgan was the Engineers Cottage, a small shingled cabin, which was her residence and headquarters while she worked on Asilomar, and later on the Hearst Castle project. The other buildings designed by Morgan that remain at Asilomar are: Stone Entrance Pillars (1913); Phoebe Apperson Hearst Social Hall, now the Administration Building (1913); Grace H. Dodge Chapel/Auditorium (1915); Mary Ann Crocker Dining Hall (1918); Visitor's Lodge (1917–18); Health Cottage, or Viewpoint (1917–18); "Stuck-Up Inn," or the Women's Residence (1918); "Pirate's Den," or the Men's Residence (1923); Director's Cottage (1927); Scripps Lodge Annex (1927–28); and Merrill Hall (1928).

Each of the residences exudes a warm and intimate atmosphere in their interiors, while retaining the overall rustic quality that is Asilomar's unifying theme. Open beamed ceilings, board-and-batten redwood paneling, stone or brick-faced fireplaces, and banded wood-casement

windows grace the lobbies of the Visitor's Lodge, Viewpoint, Stuck-Up Inn, and Pirate's Den. Stuck-Up Inn and Pirate's Den have pleasant views of their wooded surroundings, while Visitor's Lodge and Viewpoint are situated to take advantage of the wonderful ocean and shoreline vistas that are available from most of their west- and south-facing rooms.

Stuck Up Inn and the Pirate's Den were created to provide rooms for the staff at Asilomar (for the first five years, both the staff and guests stayed in tent housing and dined beneath a circus tent). The colorful names given these two residences were the result of sarcastic terms that the male and female staff had for one another. The female staff were mostly college students from fairly privileged backgrounds, who continually complained about having to do menial labor; hence the name Stuck-Up Inn. The male staff members would often raid the nearby dining hall for food between meal times; thus, their residence was labeled Pirate's Den.

The Phoebe Apperson Hearst Social Hall was the first permanent public building constructed at Asilomar. Currently known as the Administration Building, it still fulfills the purpose it was originally designed for. Guests check into their rooms at the registration desk, they

Asilomar, Pacific Grove, Merrill Hall, 1928.

ABOVE: Asilomar, Pacific Grove, Phoebe Apperson Hearst Social Hall (now Administration Building), 1913, detail of chimney. BELOW: Asilomar, Pacific Grove, Administration Building.

can entertain themselves by reading at one of the large library tables or playing pool on one of several pool tables, and there is a gift shop and snack bar at one end of the building.

The exterior of the Administration Building is clad in local fieldstone to the top of the windows, with stained redwood paneling above (which replaced the pine logs that were originally used by Julia Morgan). The banded windows are made of plateglass in casement frames that open outward to let in the fresh ocean breezes. The roofline is a low-angled, ridge-on-hip style, and is punctuated by a tall fieldstone chimney rising above the center of the eastern facade.

The interior, like all four public buildings at Asilomar designed by Julia Morgan, consists of one large open space with an impressive beamed ceiling of Douglas fir. The beams have king posts that rise to the central ridge. The walls are covered with board-and-batten, floor-to-ceiling redwood paneling. There is a large stone-faced fireplace in the center of the eastern wall, and the staff keeps a fire burning in it during the evening hours.

The Mary Ann Crocker Dining Hall has been expanded from the original central section designed by Julia Morgan, which remains intact. The main entrance of her wing faces east, and is a classic essay in Arts and Crafts architecture. The doorway is sheltered by a massive wooden pavilion, which has wide, overhanging eaves and projecting beam ends. Guests can gather here on hot or rainy days to be protected from the weather while waiting for their friends. The walls are clad in Carmel flagstone, interspersed with floor-to-ceiling banded plateglass windows. (Mary Ann Crocker, a member of San Francisco's Crocker Bank family, was not related to the famed cookbook author Betty Ann Crocker.)

Inside the Dining Hall, guests can eat in a remarkable space that evokes a baronial hunting lodge, without the stuffed animal heads. The ceiling has massive, fifty-four-foot-wide Douglas fir trusses spanning the dining area, which support an open cathedral-style roof rising twenty-five feet above the floor. This magnificent room can seat four hundred people comfortably. Dormer windows set into the slope of the roofline, and banded windows along the walls, keep the Dining Hall light despite the dark wooden beaming. Two rustic fireplaces, with fieldstone fireboxes and stained redwood paneling, grace the east and west ends of the room.[4]

The Grace H. Dodge Chapel/Auditorium has a deceptively plain exterior. At first glance, it appears to be a fairly modern structure of modest size. Reinforced concrete pillars faced with granite fieldstone support a low-angled, pent eave roofline. The banded windows along the south wall provide a direct view of the ocean a few dozen yards away.

Upon walking into the chapel, one is greeted by an unexpectedly elegant ambience in a surprisingly large space. The open-beamed Douglas fir ceiling has king posts decorated with wrought-iron bracing. The north side of the building includes built-in folding wood partitions that

Asilomar, Pacific Grove, Mary Ann Crocker Dining Hall, 1918.

can be used to divide off the north wing into classrooms during conferences. The nave of the chapel slopes gently downward, giving a clearer view of the stage from each row of seats, and creating the feeling of sitting on a sand dune. Below the clerestory windows, Julia Morgan chose to have the redwood frieze incised with gold letters that comprise two passages from the Psalms of Isaiah in the Bible. Appropriately, these passages include the following lines: "Above The Voices Of Many Waters; The Mighty Breakers Of The Sea."

The last building Julia Morgan designed at Asilomar is Merrill Hall. It is by far the largest structure she created on the conference grounds, capable of holding one thousand people at a time, although current fire safety codes have limited that number to 650. This was the largest building on the Monterey Peninsula when it was finished in 1928. Today, Merrill Hall still fulfills its multipurpose function; it is used for conferences, lectures, seminars, weddings, dances, plays, graduations, and musical concerts.[5]

ABOVE: Asilomar, Pacific Grove, Merrill Hall, 1928. FACING: Asilomar, Pacific Grove, Grace H. Dodge Chapel/Auditorium, 1915, auditorium with biblical inscription.

The exterior of Merrill Hall is unique among Julia Morgan's buildings at Asilomar, in that it incorporates historic decorative motifs. Approaching this edifice from a distance, one gets the distinct impression of a medieval great hall rising above the Monterey pines. The main facade faces west, and at the top of the wall, Morgan placed three Gothic-arched windows on each side of a massive central chimney. The chimney is faced in Carmel flagstone and rises several feet above the wide, overhanging eaves. Carmel flagstone is also used on the two tall pilasters that line each end of the main section.

Below the Gothic windows, Morgan used pine logs, now replaced with redwood paneling, and overlaid this with a half-timbered pattern. Three levels of tall wood-latticed windows fill the wall below that. The roofline of the central section has a high-peaked gable with a bargeboard, and the two side wings have steeply pitched eaves that meet the sides of the central section just below the Gothic arched windows.

The interior of Merrill Hall is truly awe inspiring. One could easily imagine having entered a thirteenth-century Gothic assembly hall for

FACING: Asilomar, Pacific Grove, Merrill Hall, auditorium. ABOVE: Asilomar, Pacific Grove, Merrill Hall, detail of ceiling.

the Knights Templar. The cathedral-style ceiling is over thirty-two feet high and is supported by two parallel rows of twenty-three-foot-long Douglas fir beams that rise to meet below the central peak of the roofline. Between these beams are open rows of Gothic arches also made of fir, four on each side of the central peak.

The walls of the two side aisles are paneled in untreated redwood, and a clerestory of Gothic arched windows lines the two sides of the central section (or nave). Just below this clerestory is a handsome frieze with carved floral patterns. At the east end of the nave is a spacious wooden stage. Above the west end of the nave is a large, multitiered choir loft. Below the choir loft, on the western wall of the building, is a walk-in fireplace, with fieldstone facing and a prehistoric fish fossil embedded in the keystone.

The genius of Julia Morgan's plan for Asilomar becomes evident after staying there for even a brief visit. As anyone who's spent a day or more in this haven can attest, this is a magical place, one that stays with you long after you've left. Asilomar does most definitely provide a "refuge by the sea"; one that refreshes the mind and soul, as well as the body.

CHAPTER 6

Academic Achievements

"El Campanil is the first reinforced concrete structure west of the Mississippi."
—Plaque on the Mills College bell tower, 1904

Being a graduate of two prestigious institutions of higher learning gave Julia Morgan a lifelong dedication to the principle that a good quality education should be made available to anyone capable of benefiting from it. Accordingly, Julia carried out some of her most distinguished commissions on behalf of academic clientele. These commissions fell into three categories: structures used by college campuses; private or specialized school buildings; and sorority houses.

One of Julia Morgan's first independent commissions, even before she had opened her own office in San Francisco, came from Mills College, a private women's college in Oakland. Mills College is the oldest women's college west of the Rockies. It was founded in 1852 in Benicia, California, a small pioneer town that was then the state capital. At that time it was called the Young Ladies Seminary. In 1866, it was renamed and moved to its current site, in the foothills of East Oakland just below the MacArthur Freeway.[1]

By 1900, the college had gained a national reputation as a highly respected private liberal arts college and had a rapidly growing student enrollment. The board of trustees decided in 1903 that it was time to begin a program of new construction, one that would reflect the college's image as a great center of higher learning and a promoter of women's achievement. Appropriately, the trustees decided to hire California's first woman architect to design several of the new structures they wanted built.

The Mills College campus covers an area of 135 acres. It projects the atmosphere of an Ivy League college on the Eastern seaboard. Rows of mature deciduous trees line many of the campus drives, and large, lush lawns are spread out between many of the academic buildings. When Julia Morgan was commissioned by the trustees in 1903 to design five new structures, all of the college functions were housed in three Victorian-era buildings.

FACING: Margaret Carnegie Library, Mills College, Oakland, Bender Room.
ABOVE: El Campanil, Mills College, Oakland, 1903–4.

The first structure Julia designed for Mills College was called "El Campanil," or "The Bell Tower." By 1900, it was a well-honored tradition for private colleges and universities in the eastern half of the United States to have a bell tower in a prominent place on campus as a symbol of the college. These bell towers were usually designed in a variation of the Gothic or Renaissance styles to evoke the conservative image of European heritage and tradition that these institutions sought to foster.

But there was nothing traditional or conservative about the bell tower Julia Morgan designed for Mills College. To start with, she decided to construct a seventy-two-foot-tall tower of undisguised reinforced concrete, which was tinted a greenish brown color to blend in with the surrounding oak and eucalyptus trees. The tower has tapered buttresses on the sides and is twice as wide as it is thick, creating an impression of being both lighter and taller than it actually is.

The style of El Campanil is Morgan's own derivation of Mission Revival. At the top is a peaked redwood gable with wide, overhanging eaves and exposed beams. Below this are three stepped arches from which several of the bells are hung. Underneath these arches is a large clock flanked by two more arches housing bells. The middle section of the facade has two more stacked arches, with the bottom one being much wider. The lower section has a covered entrance. Red clay tiles are used above this entrance, as well as on the main gable and the tops of the buttresses.

Julia placed El Campanil along one side of an elliptical lawn across from the main building on campus, the mansard-roofed Mills Hall, built in 1871. The contrast between these two edifices facing one another across the lawn, the one solid and sober, the other fanciful and ethereal, is simply wonderful to behold.

More than a visual delight, El Campanil was an engineering triumph. Morgan employed all of her recently acquired skill in working

with structural concrete on this design. After the tower was dedicated on April 14, 1904, a plaque was placed next to the front door that reads: "El Campanil is the first concrete reinforced structure west of the Mississippi." Proof of Morgan's engineering prowess can be found in the fact that neither the 1906 San Francisco earthquake, nor the 1989 Loma Prieta quake, did any damage whatsoever to this marvelous creation.

To the east of El Campanil, on the oval, is the second building Julia Morgan created for Mills College: the Margaret Carnegie Library, now known as Carnegie Hall. It was designed in 1905 and completed in 1906. The exterior of Carnegie Hall looks just as it did over a century ago—a gem of Beaux-Arts neoclassical symmetry. The facade has five tall, round-arched windows across the second story, with a wrought-iron balcony below the middle window. Below this balcony is the main entrance, and on each side of it are two sets of triple rectangular windows set into the first-floor walls. The red clay–tiled roof has wide, overhanging eaves, with a low-angled gable. Carnegie Hall was also constructed of reinforced concrete, but here Morgan used a more traditional white color.

The interior of the old library has been extensively remodeled in recent years, since the building no longer serves as the campus library. But on the second floor, the original reading room remains intact. Now called the Bender Room, this is a handsome space in the Arts and Crafts tradition. The high beamed ceiling is supported by king posts and immense wrought-iron chandeliers hang from the beams. Built-in bookshelves project at right angles from the walls, and tall pillars support rows of Romanesque columns at the top. The walls are lined with pilasters in dark-stained oak, while the tall windows bathe the room in natural light that is ideal for reading weighty tomes.

ABOVE: Margaret Carnegie Library, Mills College, Oakland, 1905–6. TOP: Ethel Moore Memorial Center, Mills College, Oakland, 1916.

North of Mills Hall, across another lush lawn, is the third facility Julia Morgan designed for the Mills campus. In 1909, she was commissioned to create a gymnasium, pool, and social hall. Today Morgan's gymnasium and pool have been almost entirely consumed by a recent expansion and remodeling. Only the original social hall remains from her design, in the annex at the southeast corner of the complex. It was completed in 1916 and originally called the Ethel Moore Memorial Center. It is currently used as the Student Union.[2] The exterior has had white paint applied to Morgan's wooden columns on the porch. The interior, however, is largely intact, with its fluted Doric columns made of redwood, boxed beamed ceilings, and rich board-and-batten wainscoting on the entry-level social hall, as well as a spacious recreation hall with an open beamed ceiling and a tall brick fireplace on the upper level.

On the west side of Kapiolani Road, across from the Fine Arts Annex, is one of the other two Julia Morgan buildings remaining on the campus. The Kapiolani Infirmary was commissioned in 1909 and built in 1910. This is a simple two-story wooden structure that originally had sleeping porches upstairs for ill or injured students to use until they recovered.

TOP: Ming Kwong Chinese Girls' School, Mills College campus, Oakland, 1924–25. ABOVE: Ming Kwong Chinese Girls' School, Mills College campus, Oakland, entry arch detail.

Phoebe Apperson Hearst Memorial Gymnasium, UC Berkeley campus, 1924–25, west entrance.

This structure was given a cosmetic updating in 2006 and was converted into an office for the campus architect.[3]

North of the main entrance to the Mills campus is a building originally designed by Morgan in 1924 as the Ming Kwong Chinese Girls' School. When it was opened in 1925, it stood on a privately owned, two-acre site next to the Mills campus. Morgan designed the school to evoke a traditional Chinese country house to provide a familiar and reassuring environment for the girls who attended here, many of whom were orphans who had been rescued from brothels or sweat shops.[4] This two-story building has a U-shaped floor plan, with the projecting wings sheltering a wide courtyard. A low wall encloses the front of this courtyard, and the arched entry gate is flanked by Chinese Fu dogs, a symbol of welcome.

The facade of the building has cast-iron balconies extending across the second story, decorated by Chinese finials and geometric patterns. Wide wood-framed doorways punctuate the first floor, with banded windows set into them to admit extra light. Below the red clay–tiled roof, there is a frieze with multicolored tiles imported from China. The authentic Chinese ambience Julia Morgan created here is yet another illustration of her adroitness in handling Asian design motifs. This building became part of the Mills campus in 1936, and for several years it was used as a conference center. In 2004, it was leased by a private girls' middle school, which remodeled parts of the interior, and now operates the facility as the Julia Morgan School for Girls.

On the UC Berkeley campus, Julia Morgan designed two very different facilities, one of them in collaboration with her mentor and former teacher, Bernard Maybeck. The older of these two structures is Girton Hall. It was designed and constructed in 1911, after a group of senior women students at Berkeley asked Morgan to design a Senior Women's Hall for their use. Girton Hall is a superb example of First Bay Tradition architecture in a busy campus setting. The exterior blends in perfectly with its natural environment, which is a low hill shaded by old redwood trees on the eastern edge of the campus (the building was moved here in the 1940s, but its original site was similarly landscaped). A low hipped roof with wide, overhanging eaves covers a simple single-story structure sheathed in redwood shingles. A wall of floor-to-ceiling windows looks out onto a redwood terrace on the west side, and banded windows on the east side flank a massive brick chimney.

The interior of Girton Hall consists of a large open room, with a beamed ceiling, redwood walls, and a brick fireplace on the eastern side. There is an enclosed porch at the south end, and a small kitchen at the north end. The building has been used since 1972 as part of the UC Berkeley Child Care Program, for which it is ideally suited. During storytelling time, when I worked there in the mid-1970s, children often looked up into the open ceiling above them and imagined monsters or fairies hiding among the rafters.

The other Julia Morgan building on the UC campus is the Phoebe Apperson Hearst Memorial Gymnasium. Originally built in 1925 as a women's gymnasium, this facility was commissioned by William Randolph Hearst as a memorial to his mother. Phoebe Hearst died in the Great Influenza Epidemic of 1919. This gymnasium was to have been part of a recreational complex that included a theater, a music hall, and a

university museum, but Hearst decided not to spend the funds needed to complete the other structures.

The Hearst Gymnasium is a masterpiece of modestly scaled Beaux-Arts design. It is one of the few collaborations between Maybeck and Morgan. The exact nature of each architect's contribution is in some dispute, but there is no doubt that the plans were worked out jointly between the two architects. Julia Morgan undoubtedly designed the three pools, since this was her forte. She also is credited with designing the series of massive reinforced concrete decorative urns that flank the main entrances. Each of these urns is festooned with a delightful growling lion's head motif. Thus, the urns bid welcome to entering students, while the lions guard against unwanted intruders.

The building itself is a sprawling two-story concrete structure, with balustraded stairways leading to the second floor at the west entrance. The windows above the west entrance are flanked by Ionic pilasters and ornamented with thin metal balusters and flower boxes embellished with swags. The pavilions at each end have equally ornate windows, but here they are bordered by columns with baroque curved gables above.

The main pool at Hearst Gymnasium is Olympic size, and Morgan placed it on the roof level to provide the students who used it with magnificent views of the East Bay Hills and the campus below. The south end of the pool has a third-story changing room with two sarcophagus-like structures in front of it, which are decorated with life-size, high-

TOP: Girton Hall, UC Berkeley campus, 1911. ABOVE: Phoebe Apperson Hearst Memorial Gymnasium, UC Berkeley campus, upper pool.

ABOVE: Phoebe Apperson Hearst Memorial Gymnasium, UC Berkeley campus, detail of cherub above upper pool. TOP, RIGHT: Phoebe Apperson Hearst Memorial Gymnasium, UC Berkeley campus, "united women" sculpture above upper pool. RIGHT: Phoebe Apperson Hearst Memorial Gymnasium, UC Berkeley campus, detail of urn at west entrance.

relief statues of united women clad in Grecian gowns carrying giant swags on their shoulders. Even more charming are the two adjacent statues of female cherubs clutching pigskins.

There is some speculation among historians, but no proof, that the reason Julia Morgan only received two commissions to design buildings on the campus of her old alma mater was jealousy on the part of John Galen Howard. As University Architect, the theory goes, he was determined not to let his former assistant outshine him. Further, some believe Howard may also have resented the fact that Morgan hired one of his best architects, Ira Wilson Hoover, in 1906 as her junior partner after she opened her own office in 1904. This assumption seems specious at best, since both of the UC buildings Julia Morgan did design were conceived and constructed before Howard retired in 1927, and would have to have received at least his tacit approval, if not his blessing. In addition, no other prominent Bay Area architects, besides Bernard Maybeck, received any commissions on the Berkeley campus while Howard was in charge.

A few blocks south of the UC Berkeley campus, where Bowditch Street intersects Dwight Way, Julia Morgan designed a handsome red brick Tudor Revival administration building for the Berkeley Baptist Divinity School. Conceived in 1918 and completed in 1920, this dignified four-story edifice has intricate decorative patterns of carved sandstone surrounding its leaded windows. The hipped roof is covered in slate and punctuated with dormer windows. The building is constructed of reinforced concrete. Attached to the north end of Hobart Hall is an attractive loggia with Gothic arches in stone, which joins Morgan's administration building to a smaller brick office building next door (not designed by Julia Morgan). The interior of Hobart Hall was retrofitted and updated in 2001 for use by its current owners, the American Baptist Seminary of the West, which retained all of Morgan's architectural features.[5]

Tudor Revival was also the style Julia Morgan chose for two other commissions near the UC Berkeley campus. The first one was the headquarters for her former sorority, Kappa Alpha Theta, at 2733 Durant Avenue. It was originally designed by Morgan in 1908 in the brown-shingled First Bay Tradition mode. Even though this building survived the disastrous Berkeley Fire of 1923, Morgan remodeled it about 1930 with a more fireproof stucco exterior in late Tudor Manor house style. Her work was almost completely lost in a heavy-handed circa-1950 "updating" of the sorority by Gardner Dailey.

TOP: Hobart Hall, Berkeley Baptist Divinity School, Berkeley (now American Baptist Seminary of the West), 1918–20. ABOVE: Hobart Hall, Berkeley, detail of rear windows.

Delta Zeta Sorority, Berkeley, living room.

One block north of the UC campus, at 2311 LeConte Avenue, Morgan designed another sorority house in 1923, for Delta Zeta. This building remains almost exactly as Morgan originally designed it. It is a three-story concrete structure, topped by a hipped roof lined with gabled dormer windows. A balcony with cast-iron railings runs across the central portion of the second story. Two sets of French doors open out onto this balcony. The ground floor has heavy beveled pillars joined by wide Tudor arches, which support the balcony above. A Tudor rose motif, in differing variations, was employed by Morgan as a repeating detail in several places along the facade: the carved panels on the front door, the capitals of the pillars, and at the tops of the rainspouts. The building is currently owned by Westminster House, which provides rooms there for students to rent.

The interior of the Delta Zeta house exhibits all the hallmarks of Julia Morgan's elegant use of historic features. An exquisite curved staircase graces the rear wall of the ground floor. The wall behind the stairwell follows the curve of the stairs, and grouped latticed windows are set into it to bathe the staircase in natural light. To the right of this staircase is a spacious dining hall, and to the left is the living room. Both rooms have large fireplaces with stone mantels embellished by heraldic motifs. All of the common rooms on the ground floor open out onto the rear patio, creating an indoor-outdoor effect that was a classic element of the First Bay Tradition.

Two private school buildings Julia Morgan designed in San Francisco illustrate the wide range of her stylistic repertoire, as well as her skill in creating institutional spaces that were ideally suited to the special needs of individual clients. The first of these is the former Methodist Chinese Mission School at 920 Washington Street in Chinatown. It was designed in 1907 and completed in 1910. Here her clients wanted a building that could house classrooms for several hundred Chinese orphans on a corner lot in a crowded urban setting. Morgan created a three-and-a-half-story clinker brick edifice with a clay tile roof. This building's floor plan makes maximum use of its limited lot space while presenting the image of a traditional Chinese masonry structure to the street.

The exterior of the Methodist Chinese Mission School incorporates a variety of Chinese motifs, including hanging lanterns and decorative tiles. The arched entrance on Washington Street has a peony motif carved into its keystone and uses this flower as a decorative pattern on the underside of the archway. A Chinese lantern hangs from the bottom of the arch. Morgan used ornamental ironwork to decorate a series of necessary fire escapes across the top floor. Today, this building is occupied by the Asian Women's Resource Center.

Across town in Pacific Heights, one of California's wealthiest and most elegant neighborhoods, Morgan employed her expertise with the Mediterranean mode in designing the Katherine Delmar Burke School. This was a college preparatory high school for girls, built in 1916 at 3025 – 3065 Jackson Street. Here, Morgan had an ample lot to work with, and decided to create a structure that integrated with the streetscape while utilizing the First Bay Tradition concept of an indoor-outdoor floor plan. The exterior of this two-story facility has pastel-colored stucco walls, red clay–tiled low-angled roofs, rounded arches, and Tuscan columns between some of the tall latticed windows, all classic Mediterranean motifs.

The main entry section of this school looks out onto a central courtyard, which is graced by a fountain and flower beds in the middle. The ground-floor classrooms, library, and main hallway all flow pleasantly together, and the rows of wide windows along both floors create a light, open feeling for all of the interior spaces. This site is now being used as the San Francisco University High School, a coeducational college preparatory school, which has kept almost all of the original Julia Morgan features.

Delta Zeta Sorority (now Westminster House), Berkeley, 1923, spiral staircase.

ABOVE: Methodist Chinese Mission School, San Francisco, 1910, doorway. FACING, TOP: Katherine Delmar Burke School (now University High School), San Francisco, 1916. FACING, BOTTOM: Katherine Delmar Burke School, San Francisco, detail of terra cotta tile work.

One other major academic design project Julia Morgan was involved with was halfway across the continent from California. This was a master plan for Principia College, a Christian Science college in the early-nineteenth-century town of Elsah, Illinois. The campus is situated atop an impressive bluff on the east side of the Mississippi, about thirty miles north of St. Louis. In 1930, Bernard Maybeck received a commission to create a new campus plan for Principia College.

Maybeck soon turned to Julia Morgan for help with this project, since his office was not large enough to handle all of the drafting of the various buildings that would be involved. Maybeck chose a combination of Elizabethan half-timbered English style for the main buildings, seventeenth-century Cotswold Cottage style for the smaller residences, and New England Greek Revival for the College Chapel. The project was never completed to Maybeck's original specifications, due to insufficient funding. Nevertheless, several dozen of his designs were built, and he and his wife, Annie, lived at the site for more than two years while construction was underway.

Julia Morgan visited the Principia College site once, in January of 1932. She sent Edward Hussey, from her office, to oversee some of the construction of the working drawings her staff produced for Maybeck's designs. But as the architectural historian Robert M. Craig clearly documents in his book *Bernard Maybeck at Principia College*, Julia Morgan's contribution to this project was that she "provided draftsmen and other assistance when Maybeck was busy, and [sic] occasionally and informally contributed suggestions and criticisms on Principia designs."[6]

CHAPTER 7

Houses of God

"Miss Julia Morgan has had charge of the construction work, and has designed all the details for the interior finish of the auditorium, and the credit for its beauty belongs to her."

—First Baptist Church of Oakland dedication program, 1908

When it came to religion, Julia Morgan's personal beliefs, as with politics, were something she did not discuss openly. There is no clear record of her having a preference for any particular religious denomination, or even of her attending church during her active career, except on special occasions. Her goddaughter, Lynn McMurray, holds that Julia was not religious at all, or at least that she did not subscribe to any organized religion. She probably attended the First Baptist Church of Oakland while she was growing up, and according to documents discovered by church historian Phillip F. Meads Jr., she definitely taught Sunday school there in the early 1890s. Indeed, her childhood home, at 754 Fourteenth Street in East Oakland, was across the corner from the original location of this church before it burned down in August of 1902.[1]

What is clear is that Julia Morgan respected and supported the important social and charitable work that churches were doing in the Bay Area during the early 1900s. She had a strong connection with the Glide Family, wealthy philanthropists from the Sacramento area who built the influential Glide Memorial Methodist Church in San Francisco. Yet Morgan was not awarded the commission to design that building, since Elizabeth Glide thought the fee she asked for her design was too high. But Julia did receive a number of commissions to design churches from her former sorority sisters at Kappa Alpha Theta in Berkeley, as well as the Mary Dodge Chapel at Asilomar in 1915 (see chapter five).

Between 1906 and 1927, Julia Morgan designed and built several churches in the Bay Area. Though their total number is not large, the stylistic variety and sophistication of design features that Morgan displayed in her church commissions make these structures some of the most interesting and original buildings of Morgan's entire career. Among the churches designed by her, those that retain their original architectural features include: the First Baptist Church of Oakland (1906–8), St. John's Presbyterian Church of Berkeley (1908–16), Thousand Oaks Baptist Church of Berkeley (1924), College Avenue United Presbyterian Church of Oakland (1917–18), High Street Presbyterian Church of Oakland (1921), First Swedish Baptist Church of Oakland, now Lakeside Baptist Church (1926), Federated Community Church of Saratoga (1923), and Ocean Avenue Presbyterian Church of San Francisco (1921), as well as a gymnasium and offices for the Hamilton Methodist Episcopal Church of San Francisco (1923).

FACING: First Baptist Church of Oakland, 1906–8. ABOVE: First Baptist Church of Oakland, 1906–8.

The First Baptist Church of Oakland was one of Julia Morgan's first independent designs after opening her own office. It is an imposing Romanesque Revival building at the northwest corner of Telegraph Avenue and 22nd Street, just north of downtown Oakland. The congregation had decided to move to this site from East Oakland in 1903, and another architect was hired to design the new building. But by the end of 1904, only the exterior walls were finished. The congregation decided to look for a new architect.

The church's leadership then commissioned Julia Morgan to design and finish the auditorium in January of 1906. She submitted a new set of plans, which were approved just before the 1906 earthquake. The quake did extensive damage to the existing church structure; the four corner towers were toppled and large sections of the outer walls had collapsed.

ABOVE: Saint John's Presbyterian Church, Berkeley, 1908–10, front entrance.
TOP: St. John's Presbyterian Church, Berkeley, detail of rear.

So Morgan was asked to rebuild the entire structure. Over the next two years, she oversaw the reconstruction of the corner towers, the gables, and the roof. She also helped choose the themes for the new stained-glass windows and picked the craftsmen who completed them.

The exterior of this building was completed by Morgan in the same Romanesque Revival style as had been planned before the earthquake. There are four massive squared corner towers with high-peaked gables rising between them, which are set into the central hipped roof. Each gable has a round stained-glass, or "rose," window. Tall windows with concentric or Romanesque-style arches punctuate the upper walls, and each has a unique stained-glass design. The upper portion of each tower has three Romanesque arches, supported by short Romanesque-style columns. The entire facade is sheathed in rusticated stone, a material that was popular for Romanesque Revival buildings to make them look weathered, like the Medieval churches in Europe by which they were inspired.

The interior of the First Baptist Church of Oakland is entirely Morgan's creation. Standing in the spacious and magnificent nave, visitors are surrounded with the aesthetic warmth and visual richness that mark the institutional work of Julia Morgan, even at this early stage of her career. The soaring hipped roof is supported by an enormous octagonal wood-framed ceiling, which has massive redwood beams projecting upward from the top of the walls to connect to a central ring of beams just below the peak. This is an ingenious engineering device, one which is both ideal for its function of supporting an unusually heavy roof spanning a large open space, while also creating a sense of historic authenticity that harmonizes with the rest of the interior.

St. John's Presbyterian Church, Berkeley, detail of ceiling.

The pews in the nave are arranged in two sets. There are curved rows of redwood seats lining the floors, while above there is an immense semi-circular balcony, which has several more rows of long curved redwood benches. All of the pews look towards a huge pipe organ set into the back wall of the church behind the altar.

The First Baptist Church of Oakland was dedicated in April of 1908. In the text of their program printed for the ceremony, the board of trustees included the following tribute to Julia Morgan's role in creating their new building:

> Miss Julia Morgan has had charge of the construction work, and has designed all the details for the interior finish of the auditorium, and the credit for its beauty belongs to her. It is the greater pleasure to pay this tribute, because of the fact that Miss Morgan was a faithful member of our Sunday school, both as pupil and teacher, and we therefore feel a special interest in the success she has achieved in her calling.[2]

St. John's Presbyterian Church of Berkeley was described in detail in chapter two. One little-known fact about this commission makes the perfection Julia Morgan achieved with this design all the more remarkable. The construction budget she was given for this church was a mere $2 per square foot! Even in the early 1900s, this was a paltry sum, since $20 per square foot was a more common figure for urban church projects of this size.[3] Clearly, Morgan was a master at turning what would have been a daunting obstacle for other architects into a triumph of creativity and ingenuity despite such severe financial restrictions.

The Thousand Oaks neighborhood of Berkeley is a pleasant area in the foothills north of the university campus, filled with charming Craftsman homes and California bungalows on quiet tree-lined streets. It was first developed in the years after the 1906 earthquake, and by the 1920s, its rapidly growing population had spawned a sizeable commercial district,

ABOVE: Thousand Oaks Baptist Church, Berkeley, sanctuary. FACING, ABOVE: Thousand Oaks Baptist Church, Berkeley, 1924. FACING, BELOW: First Swedish Baptist Church (now Lakeside Baptist Church), Oakland, 1926.

as well as several schools and churches. In 1924, Julia Morgan was commissioned to design the Thousand Oaks Baptist Church, at 1821 Catalina Street, just east of Colusa Avenue. This is a modest Mediterranean-style structure with pastel stucco walls and red clay–tiled roofs, which had a modern addition built as its west wing in the 1950s. The original 1920s section designed by Morgan retains its Italian Renaissance Revival bell tower, with round arches separated by Corinthian columns.

The interior of Thousand Oaks Baptist Church is another elegant example of Julia Morgan's skill at creating visually pleasing and impressive spaces within small structures. The area she originally designed as the nave has now been adapted for use as a theater and meeting room. It has a vaulted, open-beamed ceiling and a stage at the far end that is beautifully framed by Florentine arches and columns. Morgan gave this room a light and airy feeling with the use of tall arched windows set into the wall behind the stage.

In San Francisco, Julia Morgan designed a fine street-scale church in a working-class neighborhood that has retained all of its historic features. At 32 Ocean Avenue in the Outer Mission district stands the Ocean Avenue Presbyterian Church, just west of Mission Street. This is a colorful, multicultural area of working and lower-middle-class families, many

of them recent immigrants, much as it was in 1921 when Julia Morgan built this architectural gem of a church.

The style of the Ocean Avenue Church is Arts and Crafts with Gothic Revival detailing. The stucco and wood-trimmed exterior, which recently underwent a complete restoration, has Gothic arched windows with delicate tracery above the recessed entryway. Set into the side of the nave are pairs of tall diamond-paned leaded windows with stained glass and wood framing. Below these windows there is half-timbering, and a finely carved Celtic cross graces the low-pitched main gable. Carved into the lintel above the entrance are the words: "Faith. Hope. Love."

Perhaps the most remarkable thing about this modest church is the fact that it is still operated by its original denomination and still perfectly fulfills all of the social and cultural functions for which it was designed in 1921. Ocean Avenue Presbyterian Church provides a powerful testament to the timeless and practical qualities of Julia Morgan's church architecture.

Another superb street-scale church designed by Morgan is the College Avenue United Presbyterian Church, at 5951 College Avenue, in Oakland's upscale Rockridge district. Rockridge was first developed in the early twentieth century as a solid middle-class neighborhood surrounding the streetcar line that linked downtown Oakland to the UC Berkeley

TOP: Ocean Avenue Presbyterian Church, San Francisco, 1921, detail of gable. ABOVE: Ocean Avenue Presbyterian Church, San Francisco.

College Avenue United Presbyterian Church, Oakland, 1918.

campus. Today it is an elegant area of spacious Craftsman bungalows and two-story Colonial Revival houses.

College Avenue United Presbyterian Church was built in 1918, in a style that is primarily Arts and Crafts with some Tudor Revival features. The exterior is stucco, with a band of half-timbering across the upper walls that frames the clerestory windows. This church blends in quite well with the older two-story homes and commercial buildings that line College Avenue. The roofline has a low-angled main gable that is echoed by a small gabled cupola above. Below the gable is a large round window set into a recessed arch that continues down to the front steps. Above the entrance is a large wooden acorn, and the name of the church is carved in gilt letters just below it.

The interior is a simple but pleasant example of the Arts and Crafts style applied to a house of worship. There is a low-angled, open-beamed ceiling, and a clerestory of soft-tinted, wood-latticed windows. A shallow balcony spans the space above the entrance, which is lit by the round window set into the facade. The pipe organ along the back wall is original, as are the plain oak pews.

Across Oakland, in the working class, multiracial area of East Oakland just east of Lake Merritt, stands one of Julia Morgan's most graceful churches. Originally called the First Swedish Baptist Church, and now known as Lakeside Baptist Church, it was built in 1926 at the northwest corner of 3rd Avenue and East 15th Street. This area is known as the Brooklyn Neighborhood, and was once a separate city. Some of

Saratoga Federated Community Church, Saratoga, 1923.

Oakland's oldest and finest Victorian homes still grace the streets of this historic district.

Lakeside Baptist Church was designed in a style that blends Spanish Colonial and Renaissance Revival. It has white stucco walls and a red clay–tiled roof. Both the tall square corner tower and the recessed windows along the south facade are essentially Mission Revival. Yet the Florentine columns in the middle of each window and the neoclassical balusters lining the open belfry near the top of the tower are Renaissance details. The main gable is low angled and has heavy corbels underneath its overhanging eaves. A large Mission-style stained-glass window is set into the wall just above the main entrance, and Renaissance-style cartouches decorate the niches above the doors and all of the ground-level windows.

The interior of Lakeside Baptist Church demonstrates Julia Morgan's unrivaled skill in designing an aesthetically pleasing public space on a modest budget. The high, flat stucco ceiling is coved along the sides to create visual interest. The wall on the western side of the nave has coffered paneling and pilasters in rich wood. The eastern wall of the nave is graced by a row of five tall stained-glass windows, decorated with Art Nouveau–style borders rendered in warm yellow and red tones around deep green central panels. The overall effect is one of serenity and peaceful contemplation. This church currently serves a Chinese Baptist congregation, fulfilling its purpose just as effectively as it once did for Swedish immigrants.

In Saratoga, an affluent community about ten miles southwest of San Jose, Morgan designed the Federated Community Church in 1923. It stands at the entrance to a quiet, tree-lined lane, at 20390 Park Place. This lovely church is Julia Morgan's personal version of the Mission Revival style, with a three-story squared bell tower, red tiled roofs, and pastel stucco walls. The bell tower has three arched openings below a Moorish star motif and beveled corners on all four sides. Morgan placed three miniature balconies with wrought-iron grillwork on the front of the tower just above a tiled awning. This awning shelters the double-arched entryway, which has two massive wooden doors separated by a Corinthian pilaster, and is decorated with coffered panels. The relatively simple interior of the Saratoga Federated Community Church remains almost exactly as Julia Morgan designed it in 1923.

Saratoga Federated Community Church, Saratoga, detail of doorway.

CHAPTER 8

Of Time and Death

When she saw her completed work, she exclaimed "Oh, it's bee-you-tee-ful!"
—Marian Simpson quoting Julia Morgan at the Chapel of the Chimes, Oakland, 1928

Funerary art is a very specialized field of architecture. The clients are either the surviving family members of a recently deceased loved one or an institution that is in the business of enshrining the memory of the dead for the living to contemplate. Either way, designing funerary art requires a thoughtful combination of demonstrating sensitivity to the feelings of grieving relatives and creating appropriate tributes to the legacy of the deceased to impress future generations. Julia Morgan was superb at combining these two functions in her funerary architecture.

Julia Morgan only designed a handful of memorials to the deceased, and yet they represent some of her most visually appealing work. There are five documented sites of Morgan's funerary designs, four of them in California and one in Hawaii: the Chapel of the Chimes in Oakland (1928); a gravestone for Mr. Richard B. Ayer at Mountain View Cemetery in Oakland (1928); a marker for Mr. August F. Hockenbeamer, also at Mountain View Cemetery (1935); the Chapel of the Chimes Mortuary in Santa Rosa (1938); and the Homelani Columbarium in Hilo, Hawaii (1935).

The Chapel of the Chimes is one of California's greatest treasures of funerary art. The name refers to a rare example of a large complex that combines a memorial chapel, a columbarium, a mausoleum, private meeting rooms, and offices. The main entrance to the Chapel of Chimes complex is at 4499 Piedmont Avenue in Oakland, at the end of a quiet cul-de-sac just south of the gates to Mountain View Cemetery. Around the corner, at Pleasant Valley Road and Howe Street, is the oldest part of the complex, the Oakland Memorial Columbarium, which was built in 1902. (A columbarium is a mausoleum that displays the enclosed and shelved remains of the deceased in a rotunda-shaped building.) By the 1920s, the space within the Oakland Columbarium was rapidly filling up, and the directors decided they needed to expand their facilities.

Julia Morgan was hired in 1926 to design a memorial chapel, a new mausoleum, meeting rooms, and offices that would face Piedmont Avenue. She chose to use a blend of Romanesque and Gothic features, a combination that was used during the thirteenth century in Italy, when these two styles overlapped. The handsome sand-colored stone and concrete facade on each one of these connected buildings, which Morgan completed in 1928, was embellished with Venetian Gothic–style tracery over all the doors and windows. The name "Chapel of the Chimes" has come to be used as the term for the entire complex, both the Julia Morgan–designed section and those built later behind it.[1]

FACING: Chapel of the Chimes, Oakland, archway with niches. ABOVE: Chapel of the Chimes, Oakland, chapel wing.

FACING: Chapel of the Chimes, Oakland, gothic loggia. ABOVE: Chapel of the Chimes, Oakland, 1926–28, view of complex along Piedmont Avenue. BELOW: Chapel of the Chimes, Oakland, gothic loggia detail.

The Piedmont Avenue facade of the Chapel of Chimes complex bears the influence of Julia Morgan's Beaux-Arts training. The horizontal plane of the complex is divided by four projecting pavilions: the Chimes Chapel, two Gothic covered porches that serve as the main entrances, and the general offices. The Chimes Chapel consists of a nave with a low-angled gabled roof and two attached side aisles. The roofs of the entire Julia Morgan complex are covered in red clay tiles. An authentic-looking Romanesque bell tower rises over the left rear corner of the chapel, reminiscent of small churches in the hill towns of Tuscany.

The interior of the Chimes Chapel combines beautiful details and deep, rich colors to create an overall ambience of peace and quiet contemplation. A series of four concrete Gothic arches span a beamed ceiling, which is made of hand-hewn wood. Dividing the side aisles from the nave are Gothic columns that support intricate Venetian Gothic tracery. Set into the upper walls of the nave are rose windows with lovely stained glass in colors of deep blue and yellow, offset with rich orange.

At the west end of the nave is a large Gothic arch filled by openwork tracery, with a narrow balcony in front of it, which overlooks the coffin viewing area. Behind the tracery is a decorative screen of stained glass with the same colors as the rose windows. Above the east end of the nave is a wide balcony with a large pipe organ that is framed by Gothic tracery. The outer walls of the side aisles have tall lead-latticed windows that admit a soft natural light.

ABOVE: Chapel of the Chimes, Oakland, interior of the chapel. FACING, ABOVE: Chapel of the Chimes, Oakland, domed passageway. FACING, BELOW LEFT: Chapel of the Chimes, Oakland, Chapel of the Psalm. FACING, BELOW RIGHT: Chapel of the Chimes, Oakland, Chapel of the Holy Word.

The rest of the interior of the Julia Morgan section of the Chapel of the Chimes is an enchanting array of stained-glass atriums, domed courts, cloistered gardens, small chapels, and Gothic hallways, all arranged in ascending terraces that climb the gentle upslope site. The ambience here is somewhat reminiscent of the Alhambra Palace Gardens in Grenada, Spain. The names of some of these chapels and courts are indicative of the care and sensitivity that Julia brought to designing funerary art. She created a total of seventy-nine chapels, courts, and cloisters in her portion of the complex.[2]

The Chapel of the Psalm, for instance, has a beautifully rendered painting on canvas on its rear wall embellishing the words to the Lord's Prayer. Another lovely chapel is the Chapel of the Holy Word, which has a marvelous cathedral ceiling with rich yellow, blue, and orange panes of stained glass set into Gothic tracery and a della Robbia of the Virgin Mary gracing the back wall. The names of some the other chapels and gardens include: Everlasting Life, Everlasting Praise, The Blessed, Loving Kindness, Gentle Spirit, Consolation, Constancy, Confidence, Memory, Serenity, Peace, Promise, Courage, Strength, Truth, Trust, Fidelity, Mercy, Patience, Comfort, Eternal Wisdom, Refuge, Dignity, Grace, Hope, and Love. Each one of these spaces evokes a sense of timeless beauty, fulfilling Morgan's intention to offer relatives of the deceased much solace when contemplating the loss of a loved one.

Morgan's use of stained glass in the main chapel and in the adjacent wings of the mausoleum brightens what are often dark and dreary spaces in other funeral homes. This stained glass was largely the work of one of Julia's most trusted craftsmen, Mrs. Marian Simpson. When she saw her completed work, she exclaimed, "Oh, it's bee-you-tee-ful!"

ABOVE: Chapel of the Chimes, Oakland, fountain detail. ABOVE, RIGHT: Chapel of the Chimes, Oakland, gothic tracery on facade.

The entrance to Mountain View Cemetery is located at the north end of Piedmont Avenue in Oakland, within sight of the front of the Chapel of the Chimes. It is one of the oldest and most beautiful cemeteries in Northern California, and its more than two hundred acres make it one of the largest burial grounds in the Bay Area. This cemetery was organized in 1863, and its grounds were designed by America's first great landscape architect, Frederick Law Olmsted, who designed New York's Central Park. Within the grounds of Mountain View Cemetery is an impressive collection of thousands of monuments, grave markers, and crypts, which run the gamut of styles that were popular in nineteenth- and twentieth-century America.

Julia Morgan designed two gravestones in Mountain View Cemetery for former clients. These were for Mr. Richard Bartlett Ayer, a wine merchant for whom she had designed a residence in Piedmont California in 1914 (see chapter eleven), and for Mr. August Frederick Hockenbeamer, for whom she had designed a residence in Berkeley in 1913. These gravestones stand a few yards apart, in the southeast corner of Lot 4, near the center of the cemetery. Both of these markers have an appealing modesty and grace to their designs.

The Ayer gravestone was designed in 1928 and is the smaller of the two. It consists of a light gray granite rectangular slab about five feet tall, with a two-tiered base, a slanted top, and projecting slabs along both sides. It is essentially Streamlined Moderne in style, which was a more modest version of Art Deco. There are four-leaf clover patterns in the upper corners, with incised lines running down from them. The name "AYER" is carved in large capital letters into the center of the stone, with the names of Richard and other family members above the base.

The Hockenbeamer gravestone is also in the Streamlined Moderne style. It was designed in 1935, and is made from a large gray granite rectangular slab, about six feet high, with dark gray strips along the bottom and on the base. Indented geometric patterns in the upper corners, with rose blossom motifs, frame the name "HOCKENBEAMER" in the center of the stone. Projecting slabs line both edges of the marker, and the names of August and other family members are engraved near the bottom.

Julia Morgan also designed a "Retiring Building" for Mountain View Cemetery. It was built in 1907 and was used to provide grieving relatives with a quiet, private place to be alone with their thoughts and memories of a deceased loved one or to gather before or after a funeral service. It was demolished in the 1950s.

Ayer Gravestone, Mountain View Cemetery, Oakland, 1928.

Santa Rosa is one of the oldest towns in Northern California, and the largest city between San Francisco and Portland. Much of the late-nineteenth- and early-twentieth-century core of the town remains, including the Victorian neighborhood that Alfred Hitchcock used as a setting for his classic 1946 film, *Shadow of a Doubt*.

In the 1930s, Santa Rosa was still a sleepy, bucolic small town, with farm fields and vineyards within sight of downtown. In 1938, Julia Morgan was asked to design a new mausoleum near the southern edge of town. It was originally called Chapel of the Chimes Mortuary, and is currently known as the Neptune Society of Santa Rosa. The site of the facility, at 2607 Santa Rosa Avenue, was surrounded by fruit orchards and truck farms in the 1930s.[3]

According to Lynn McMurray, Julia Morgan started the design for the Chapel of the Chimes Mortuary, but after a preliminary drawing, she turned the project over to one of her draftsmen, George Nussbaum. Thus, no one can be certain how much of the final design Morgan was responsible for. But she did create the overall concept for the facility.

The plan of Santa Rosa's Chapel of the Chimes is simple yet elegant. It consists of a long facade facing Santa Rosa Avenue, with three projecting pavilions. The style of this complex is Spanish Colonial Revival with some Mission Revival details. The exterior walls are surfaced in pastel-colored stucco, and the roof is covered in red clay tiles. The center pavilion has a two-story tower above a porte cochere. This porch is supported by clasping buttresses at the corners and has plastered arches textured to look like wood. A low-pitched gable rises behind the tower, at the front end of a small chapel.

The south and north pavilions are a single story, with low-pitched gables. There is a shallow portico on the northern pavilion, and a wooden-beamed projecting porch on the southern one. Both of these smaller pavilions have porthole windows below the gables, and the window on the north pavilion has a pointed star motif, reminiscent of Spanish California Missions.

The interior of the Santa Rosa Chapel of the Chimes resembles a lighter, simpler, more open version of the Oakland Chapel of the Chimes. It consists of a series of atriums, with gabled skylights that admit lots of natural light to illuminate the memorial niches in the walls below. There are rose windows set into the gables of some of these rooms, with delicate stained-glass panes.

A small chapel inside the central pavilion has delicate stained-glass windows in blue, yellow, and orange, which are decorated with symbols from Christianity and Judaism: a menorah, a Star of David, and "The Lamb

Homelani Columbarium, Hilo, Hawaii, 1935–37. Photo by Mark A. Wilson.

of God." Just behind this chapel, on a stucco wall facing it, is an especially lovely della Robbia that depicts the Virgin Mary praying over the baby Jesus. There is an open courtyard between the 1930s section of the complex and the rear portion, which was added later by other architects.

Hilo is a small city on the east coast of the big island of Hawaii, at the southern end of the Hawaiian Islands. Julia Morgan's design for the Oakland Chapel of the Chimes was so greatly admired throughout the United States that when the Congregational Church in Hilo decided in 1930 to build a columbarium on the grounds of their own cemetery, the head of the building committee traveled to the Oakland Columbarium to see for himself if it lived up to its reputation. After he had visited Morgan's masterpiece, he went straight to her office and immediately commissioned her to design the new Homelani Columbarium in Hilo.

The final set of working drawings for the columbarium in Hilo was not approved until 1935, and construction on the project was completed in 1937.[4] The style Morgan chose to use was a simplified version of Mediterranean, with pastel stucco walls and green clay tiles covering a set of low-gabled roofs. The overall design consists of a long, low horizontal mass, with a porte cochere for hearses connected to the front-entry pavilion. Streamlined Moderne–style vertical panels are set into the walls between tall multipaned windows. These windows are shaded by an openwork, fish-scale pattern made out of decorative tiles. A Star of David motif was part of Morgan's original design for the upper surface of the archway on the interior of the entry pavilion. The effect created by Morgan's design for the Homelani Columbarium is one of dignity and serenity, and this facility has been declared a Hawaii State Landmark.

CHAPTER 9

Quiet Corners of Commerce and Culture

Above the doorway to the shop, Suppo placed an ornate carved wood plaque that had a basket of flowers at the top,
and the words "J. Suppo, Wood Carving, Furniture, Made to Order."

—Jules Suppo Shop and Apartments, San Francisco, 1925

Designing "quiet corners" for commerce or culture in the middle of a busy urban environment was something Julia Morgan was especially adept at. She managed to create an aesthetically pleasing ambience in both her commercial and social commissions, which was conducive to the purposes of such buildings. Julia's designs provided a shop owner, a newspaper editor, a hotel manager, or a theater director with a setting for their work that was inspirational as well as practical.

One of Julia Morgan's most loyal clients was an Oakland entrepreneur named Fred C. Turner. Mr. Turner commissioned a house from her in 1907, at 255 Ridgeway Avenue in Oakland (see chapter eleven). He later hired Morgan to design two small, street-scale shopping centers, which are still in use today; at Piedmont Avenue and 40th Street in North Oakland in 1916, and on Bancroft Avenue east of Telegraph Avenue near the UC Berkeley campus, in 1938.

The Fred Turner Shops in Oakland are a cherished landmark in the historic upscale district known as the Piedmont Avenue Neighborhood. This elegant brick-faced complex has a series of bays along the ground floor that house small shops and restaurants, and a few apartments on the second story. The basic style of the edifice is Renaissance Revival, with the total symmetry of the street facade, a low-angled gable on the second story, and porthole windows set into the brick walls, which are bordered by della Robbia–type terra cotta decorative patterns of fruits and vegetables. Stepping into one of the boutique shops or gourmet cafes on the ground floor, customers are surrounded by an atmosphere that is reminiscent of such neighborhood establishments in the historic towns of Italy.

The Turner Shops in Berkeley are located at 2552 through 2546 Bancroft Avenue, across the street from the UC Berkeley campus. This commercial complex consists of a one-story, street-scale structure with boutique shops and cafes arranged around a central light court. Originally it housed a popular bistro called the Black Sheep Restaurant, which closed many years ago. The interior of the building has been extensively remodeled in recent years, but much of Morgan's exterior remains.

The street facade has two wide side bays flanking the entrance. These bays have metal latticed windows and doors, and they are decorated with a Streamlined Moderne "curtain molding" pattern in copper as a frieze along the top, with sunburst motifs at the corners. The entryway has a curved arch over a metal-latticed glass screen that leads into the central courtyard. The walls are made of sand-colored, textured concrete, and the roof is covered in red clay tiles. The rear portion of the building has a second story, with offices and storerooms. The complex currently houses variety shops and eateries that cater to the college crowd. Julia Morgan also designed a laboratory facility and a medical building for Fred Turner on Bancroft Way in 1938, but both buildings were demolished after WWII.

FACING: Sacramento Public Market, Sacramento, neoclassic details above entrance.
ABOVE: Fred Tuner Shops and Apartments, Oakland, 1916.

Across the Bay in San Francisco, Morgan created a unique shop and residence for one of her most valued craftsmen. Jules Suppo was a woodcarver and engraver from Switzerland. He did much of the woodwork for Hearst Castle at San Simeon and for the Hearst Retreat at Wyntoon. He did not want to move his family out of San Francisco during these projects, so Julia designed a combined workshop and apartment house for him in 1925, at 2423–2425 Polk Street, in the relatively quiet Russian Hill district. The structure she created is a gem of Renaissance Revival craftsmanship that evokes the small family-owned restaurants and shops in towns like Lugano, Switzerland.

The Jules Suppo Shop and Apartment is a two-story wood-frame building, with a workshop and salesroom on the ground floor and the family residence above. There are two entrances on the street level, one for his family and one for the shop. The exterior of this edifice was designed to provide Jules Suppo with an ideal showcase for his superb woodworking talents.

Above the doorway to the workshop, Suppo placed an ornate carved wood plaque that had a basket of flowers at the top and the words "J. Suppo, Wood Carving, Furniture, Made to Order" below. A second plaque above the door to his family's apartment had two birds fluttering above a bowl of fruit, and a bouquet of flowers above them. The two doors were even more ornate: the door to his shop was encrusted with delicately carved animals, birds, and fish set into an intricate lacework pattern, while the door to his apartment was decorated with Renaissance-style coffered panels with floral and vine motifs.

ABOVE: Fred Turner Shops and Apartments, Oakland, detail of della Robbia. ABOVE, RIGHT: Jules Suppo Shop and Apartment, San Francisco, 1925.

On the second story Morgan placed an ornate balustraded balcony, which has three tall windows opening onto it from the apartment. Below this balcony were four brackets, which Suppo decorated with the faces of children eating fruit. At the top of the second story, just below a wide cornice line, there was a frieze that was carved with angels and garlands, interspersed with shields that displayed the symbols of Switzerland and Suppo's home canton.

In the heart of downtown San Francisco, at the southeast corner of 3rd and Market streets, Julia Morgan did some major remodeling for the Hearst Building. The building housed the flagship Hearst newspaper, the *San Francisco Examiner*. This twelve-story steel-frame building had been built in 1909, and was designed by the San Francisco firm of Kirby, Petit, and Green.[1] In 1937, William Randolph Hearst commissioned Morgan to design some much-needed upgrading of the interior, as well as a much more ornamental entrance and lobby.

Morgan's design for the new entrance reflects the monumental ego of the media mogul who owned the building. A two-story Baroque marble pediment supported by ornate pilasters frames the entryway, with a giant

TOP: Jules Suppo Shop and Apartment, San Francisco, detail of carved birds. ABOVE, LEFT: Jules Suppo Shop and Apartment, San Francisco, detail of wooden sign. ABOVE, RIGHT: Jules Suppo Shop and Apartment, San Francisco, detail of balcony.

ABOVE: Potrero Hill Neighborhood House, San Francisco, 1921, view of entry hall. FACING: Hearst Examiner Building, San Francisco, 1937, detail of main entrance.

letter "H" emblazoned on a mammoth cartouche at the top. Above the doors is a bronze frieze with the words "Hearst Building," and a tall metal screen decorated with animals of the forest fills the space between the pilasters.

The Hearst Building is on one of the busiest corners in San Francisco, but as soon as you step into the lobby, you leave the noise and commotion of the city behind. The two-story open foyer is lined in cool, earth-toned marble, producing an immediate calming effect. Upstairs, several of the offices were enlarged and lightened, and a state-of-the-art broadcasting station was added to serve the growing demand for instant news.

The Potrero Hill neighborhood of San Francisco is on the eastern edge of the City by the Bay, between the Mission district and Hunters Point.

This district is a mixture of gentrified homes and apartments lining the slopes of Potrero Hill, and working-class bungalows on the flatlands below. Nestled into the ridge of the hill between these two worlds is one of Julia Morgan's finest and most versatile cultural facilities: the Potrero Hill Neighborhood House.

Located at 953 De Haro Street, the Potrero Hill Neighborhood House was designed in 1921 on another part of the hill, and moved ninety feet north to its current lot in 1924.[2] Morgan's original design was a single-story, multilevel Arts and Crafts–style structure, with a low-sloping roofline and shingles and clapboards covering the walls. When the building was moved to its current site, Morgan's features and environmentally sensitive plan were retained almost intact. The center embraces its

HEARST · BUILDING ·

5

ABOVE: Native Daughters of the Golden West, San Francisco, 1927–29, facade.
ABOVE, RIGHT: Native Daughters of the Golden West, San Francisco, detail of crest above entrance, with California bears.

steep lot as though it were part of the landscape, demonstrating Morgan's continuing affinity for nature-based design in her later First Bay Tradition work.

The interior also displays all of the basic elements of the First Bay Tradition. The entry hall has board-and-batten redwood paneling lining the walls and an Early American–style fireplace, with earth-toned tile facing. To the right of it is an auditorium and theater, which has an open-beamed, low-pitched ceiling. This room takes full advantage of its natural setting, with a breathtaking view of the bay from the plateglass picture windows along its eastern wall. The Potrero Hill Neighborhood House has continued to serve its original purpose as a multiuse neighborhood cultural center for more than eighty-five years. It is now listed as an official San Francisco City Landmark.

The Native Daughters of the Golden West is a social and cultural organization of native-born California women who are "dedicated to the preservation of California history and the social and cultural development of their state." This order was founded in 1886 as an offshoot of the Native Sons of the Golden West. The Native Daughters conduct a wide variety of social and cultural activities, including a Children's Foundation to pay for the medical needs of deserving children, a Scholarship Fund for California college students, the restoration and preservation of California's Spanish Missions, and the researching and documentation of California history.[3]

The San Francisco Chapter of the NDGW was founded in 1898, and like most chapters, it maintained a residence and cultural center for its members. Their original home was a rented house, and they subsequently

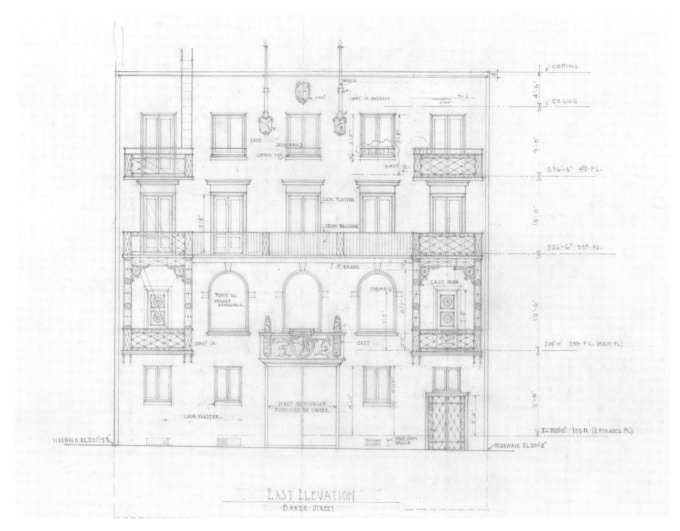

Native Daughters of the Golden West, San Francisco, front elevation (note Julia Morgan's phonetic spelling of "wrought").
Courtesy of CED, UC Berkeley.

purchased a residence that was destroyed in the 1906 earthquake. After moving to a second house on Baker Street in 1913, the board decided to demolish that home and hire Julia Morgan to design a larger permanent center for the chapter in 1927. Construction on the new home began on June 18, 1928, and the center was dedicated in January 1929. The total construction cost was $91,000.[4]

The San Francisco NDGW Center is a four-story concrete-and-steel structure at 555 Baker Street, two blocks north of the Golden Gate Park Panhandle, in the Western Addition. The style of the building is primarily Renaissance Revival, with California details. There is intricate wrought-iron grillwork around the ground-floor windows and over the front door. Above the recessed entry porch is a stucco bas-relief crest with the NDGW logo, flanked by a state flag and California grizzly bears.

The lobby is framed by Renaissance arches with Corinthian columns. The beamed ceiling has Arts and Crafts painted patterns, and there is a fireplace with California poppies in a monogram decorating the mantel. At the far end of the lobby, set on a lower level, is an auditorium that is used as a meeting hall for the chapter. On the three floors above are twenty-four residence rooms, with a multipurpose lounge and dining area on the third level.

The lounge has a fireplace with Italian Renaissance columns in stone below the mantel. This quiet, comfortable parlor was designed to be used as a library and reading room, as well as a sitting room and meeting place. Adjoining the parlor is a sunlit patio, with a large atrium above and Renaissance arches bordering it on three sides. The dining room has an impressive fireplace, with a California grizzly bear carved onto the keystone set into a stone mantel. The entire dining area has a light, airy feeling, providing members and their guests with a refuge from the noise and commotion of San Francisco's streets just two stories below. The NDGW Center is currently not being occupied as a permanent residence home, but the rooms can be used for members and their guests to stay for short visits at a subsidized rate. The common areas of the building are now used as a Public Reference Library, a Historic House Museum, a meeting hall, and administrative offices.

In Palo Alto, at 27 University Avenue, across the street from the Stanford campus, Julia Morgan converted a former Southern Pacific railroad depot into a YWCA Hospitality Center in 1919–20. The building has a simple, board-and-batten exterior with latticed windows. But the interior is surprisingly spacious, with a soaring, open-beamed ceiling supported by cross-struts, and rustic redbrick fireplaces at each end with wide balconies above. The original Art Nouveau, delicate, wrought-iron chandeliers still hang from the ceiling. This structure now houses the upscale MacArthur Park Restaurant.

RIGHT: YWCA Hospitality Center (now MacArthur Park Restaurant), Palo Alto, 1919–20, front entrance. BELOW: YWCA Hospitality Center, Palo Alto, interior.

Sacramento Public Market (now Sheraton Grand Hotel), Sacramento, 1923.

Sacramento is more than the capital of California. It is a thriving modern city with over 450,000 residents that has maintained its historic center dating back to the early days of the California Gold Rush. During the early 1920s, Sacramento was a much smaller and quieter community, with about 70,000 inhabitants.[5] But it had civic boosters, like Mrs. Elizabeth Glide, who foresaw a grander, more cosmopolitan future for their city. In 1923, Mrs. Glide commissioned Julia Morgan to design a new Sacramento Public Market, at 1230 J Street, about one-half mile from the state capitol building.

There had been an informal farmers' market at this same location in downtown Sacramento since the late 1800s. But Mrs. Glide believed the growing city deserved a more permanent and elegant facility, befitting the capital of the greatest agriculture-producing state in the nation. The lot she chose for Morgan to design the new Public Market sits at a busy corner, with wide sidewalks setting it back from the street. Julia's plan used this factor to great advantage, placing the main entrance of the building at a diagonal to the corner, which creates the feeling of a more formal transition from the bustling street to the ordered space for commerce within the structure.

The Sacramento Public Market is one of the most elegant commercial buildings in the western United States. This redbrick, two-story edifice is an understated version of the Beaux-Arts style, with refined neoclassical detailing along the exterior, and the steel-framed structure clearly visible on the interior. The facade is decorated with Ionic brick pilasters topped by terra cotta capitals, which frame a series of wide factory-sash windows on the second story. Above the entrance is a Renaissance motif in terra cotta of tall volutes supporting a garland made of fruits and vegetables.

The interior of this Public Market is at once boldly functional and aesthetically serene. There is a spacious central open area with natural light pouring in from the second-story clerestory windows. Morgan's original floor plan had stalls and shops arranged along the ground floor, which were separated by wooden partitions. A wide balcony encircles the upper story, and Morgan left the steel columns and braces that support the ceiling open to view. Ornate wooden balusters with urn designs and flower boxes graced the outer edge of the balcony.

During the 1960s and '70s, the Sacramento Public Market underwent a number of changes in use, including retail stores and a sports arena.

Sacramento Public Market (now the Sheraton Grand Hotel lobby), view of interior. Photo courtesy of Sheraton Grand Hotel.

In 1979, the State of California bought the building and, as part of the then-new trend toward adaptive reuse of historic buildings, it remodeled the interior to house the Secretary of State's offices. Some design changes were made at that time, such as enclosing much of the balcony area with glass-fronted offices.

In 2001, the interior of the Public Market was remodeled once again for its current use as the lobby and reception area for the Sheraton Grand Hotel, which caters to tourists and visitors conducting business with the state government. The old balcony, metal beams, and skylights were opened up to view once again in this recent renovation. The ground floor is now occupied by the registration desk, bar, and Morgan Cafe, with a new ballroom installed below street level. The balcony area contains a restaurant at one end and several meeting rooms at the opposite end. The building's original historic exterior remains intact, an eloquent reminder of Sacramento's early-twentieth-century vision of itself as a future cosmopolitan center of commerce and culture.

924 Anacapa Street, between Carillo and Canon Perdido streets, just west of the old Spanish Presidio. Today, the structure houses a private residential club and is known as the Lobero Building.

The exterior of the Margaret Baylor Inn has a subtle, understated elegance. Its four-story whitewashed facade has a Mission-arched entrance, with two tall, round-arched windows at the street level. Across the top floor, Morgan placed a long recessed balcony with simple concrete pilasters between each section to provide privacy for the guests who occupied these penthouse rooms. Above the main entrance, she designed a more decorative Spanish Colonial wrought-iron balcony, with delicate tracery patterns along the railings. The recessed front doorway is composed of two tall glass-and-oak-paneled doors that lead into a richly embellished formal lobby lit by a large fanlight transom. Today, more than eighty years after it was built, this building still provides its residents and staff with a quiet and charming environment in which to live and work.

San Luis Obispo is a bucolic town on California's Central Coast that began its history as a Spanish Mission in 1772. Its population grew steadily after the Southern Pacific Railroad arrived in 1894. By the late 1920s, the town had become a popular vacation destination for visitors from both Northern and Southern California who were seeking a respite from big-city life and wanted a convenient place to stay while they explored the Central Coast.

In 1925, a group of six women from San Luis Obispo decided to form a club in order to "promote the cultural, civic, and social welfare of the community." They called themselves the Monday Club and, for the first few years, they met every Monday in the basement of the old city library. In 1928, one of the members who had seen the plans Julia Morgan drew

ABOVE: Margaret Baylor Inn (now Lobero Building), Santa Barbara, 1925–26. Photo by Mark A. Wilson. BELOW: Monday Club, San Luis Obispo, 1933–34.

Santa Barbara is one of California's oldest and loveliest cities. It was first settled by the Spanish in 1782 as a fortress, and its jewel of a mission was founded in 1786. The old city lies along the peaceful shores of Santa Barbara Bay, facing the deep blue waters of the Pacific Ocean, with the mountains of the Los Padres National Forest behind it. Downtown Santa Barbara retains numerous remnants of its Spanish Colonial and Mexican past, with dozens of adobe buildings from the late eighteenth and early nineteenth centuries. The business and civic center consists mostly of Spanish Colonial Revival–style structures built in the 1920s and '30s, with whitewashed stucco walls and red clay–tiled roofs.

In 1925, Julia Morgan was commissioned to design a residential hotel in downtown Santa Barbara called the Margaret Baylor Inn. This handsome Spanish Colonial Revival hotel was completed in 1926. It stands at

ABOVE: Los Angeles Examiner Building, detail of balcony. FACING: Los Angeles Examiner Building, 1915.

for the Berkeley Women's City Club suggested that the Monday Club retain Julia Morgan to design a permanent clubhouse for them. Julia was traveling to San Luis Obispo regularly at the time to supervise the construction of Hearst Castle at San Simeon, about forty-five miles to the north. In lieu of a fee, she agreed to design the clubhouse in exchange for free room and board whenever she was passing through town. It took the members five years to raise the funds for construction. Morgan drew up the plans in 1933, and the clubhouse was dedicated on May 11, 1934.[6]

The Monday Club stands at 1800 Monterey Street, on the edge of an early-twentieth-century residential neighborhood. The single-story Spanish Colonial building is set well back from the street, with a wide lawn in front of it. The pastel stucco walls and low-gabled, red clay–tiled roof are classic Spanish Colonial features. But Morgan added a note of neoclassical sophistication to the building by making the main entrance a tall, round-arched doorway, with a keystone above the wide transom. The entry pavilion is flanked by Tuscan-like columns, which are also placed at the corners of the main structure. The use of vigas, or exposed beam ends, underneath the corners of each of the four gables provides a touch of historic authenticity.

The interior of the Monday Club has a grand auditorium with a stage, used as a meeting site and performance and lecture hall. The ceiling of

this hall is high-peaked, supported by open beams with massive king posts. Along the walls are original murals drawn by one of Julia Morgan's favorite artists, Doris Day. Morgan chose the sylvan theme for these murals, a series of loquat trees common to San Luis Obispo, which she enjoyed the fragrance of whenever she visited the town.[7]

Los Angeles in 1910 was still a small city, with about 320,000 people, little more than half the population of the state's largest city at that time, San Francisco. But during the next decade, Los Angeles would experience explosive growth, nearly doubling its population to almost 600,000 by 1920.[8] William Randolph Hearst was well aware of the growing importance of Los Angeles as a media market during the 1910s. So in 1915, he decided to build a new headquarters and printing plant for the local Hearst newspaper, the *Los Angeles Examiner*, and he hired his mother's favorite architect to design it, Julia Morgan.

The Examiner Building stands intact on the southeastern fringes of downtown Los Angeles. It occupies an entire city block, along Broadway between 11th and 12th streets.

The style of this romantic-looking, four-story structure is a tour-de-force in the Mission Revival mode, with a heavy emphasis on Moorish detailing. It was clearly inspired by the California Pavilion at the 1893 Columbian Exposition in Chicago, which was designed by prominent San Francisco architect A. Page Brown, and had been one of the most popular buildings at that fair. The California Pavilion helped start the Mission Revival movement, which spread throughout the United States between the 1890s and the 1930s.

That the Mission Revival style was one of Julia Morgan's favorite modes in her wide repertoire is evident when one looks up at the impressive facade of the Examiner Building. A Mission-style arcade runs the entire length of the building on the street level. Along the second story, ornate wrought-iron grillwork decorates the wide, triple-framed windows. Above these windows, Morgan placed wide, overhanging eaves with heavy viga-like brackets.

The central pavilion of the structure has an Espanada, or Spanish Baroque gable, with a Moorish pointed star window above the arched front entrance. Flanking the gable are twin three-story mock bell towers with blue-and-yellow-tiled domes. Rising above the entire edifice is a four-story central tower with a rotunda topped by a cupola. This tower has loggias along the front and sides, covering open balconies. At all four corners of the building, three-story towers support domes with intricate patterns of blue and yellow tiles. The roofs of each section are covered in red clay tiles, and the entire facade is sheathed in pastel yellow stucco.

FACING: Los Angeles Examiner Building, front arcade and corner tower. ABOVE: Los Angeles Examiner Building, detail of dome with glazed tile.

The lobby of the Examiner Building carries the Spanish-Baroque/Moorish theme to even more impressive heights. The high ceiling has massive wooden beams, from which hang opulent chandeliers. The floors are covered in decorative patterned tiles, and on the walls and columns are baroque bas-relief panels in terra cotta. Two series of wide, tall arches span the center section of this spacious room, and sumptuous, Renaissance-style staircases ascend toward the second floor from each side of the lobby. Julia Morgan did some remodeling of the upstairs interior in 1921 and 1930.

At this writing, the Examiner Building sits empty, awaiting a developer with vision to give it new life. It was after his collaboration with Julia Morgan on this Mission Revival masterpiece that William Randolph Hearst began to envision, during the spring of 1919, something much grander being created on his ranch at San Simeon; a baronial estate that would capture the world's attention and come to be known as "Hearst Castle."

CHAPTER 10

The Hearst Connection

"I would like to build something up on the hill at San Simeon. I get tired of going up there and camping in tents. I'd like to get something that would be a little more comfortable."

—William Randolph Hearst to Julia Morgan in her office, 1919

There could not have been two more disparate personalities—or so it seemed at first glance; the bear-like, gregarious, ego-driven media mogul, and the petite, reserved, self-effacing architect. But in truth, William Randolph Hearst and Julia Morgan had more in common than casual observers could ever imagine. Both were fiercely devoted to their work, both were dreamers who knew how to make their dreams come to life, and both had an unshakable determination to succeed in the face of daunting odds. They had the same level of boundless energy, an uncommon ability to focus on the task at hand, and great creativity. During their twenty-eight-year-long collaboration on Hearst's compound at San Simeon, it was clear to the hundreds of people who saw them work together that they had enormous respect for one another and a genuine affection born of seeing a shared vision take shape.

There is no definite record of how and when William Randolph Hearst and Julia Morgan first met, but it was probably at his mother Phoebe's country villa in Pleasanton, California, Hacienda del Pozo de Verona, on which Morgan did extensive remodeling and construction between 1903 and 1910. In any case, they had collaborated on two projects before the Los Angeles Examiner Building. In 1912, Hearst had asked Morgan to design a mansion for him in Sausalito, atop a steep hillside above San Francisco Bay. The residence was never built, but Julia did design a massive retaining wall that still stands intact nearly a century later. Then, in 1914, Morgan designed a vacation cottage for Hearst on the South Rim of the Grand Canyon (the cottage was demolished about 1950). These three projects were enough to convince Hearst of Julia's considerable engineering skills, which would be severely tested in the construction of his country estate at San Simeon.

The nucleus of the Hearst Ranch at San Simeon had been purchased by William Randolph's father, George Hearst, in 1865, when his son was

FACING: Hearst Castle, Casa Grande, South Gothic Suite. ABOVE: William Randolph Hearst and Julia Morgan during the construction of Hearst Castle, photographed by film director Irvin Willat in 1926. Courtesy of Bison Archives.

two years old. George had originally purchased forty thousand acres, but he bought up more adjoining land over the next quarter of a century. William continued this habit after his father's death in 1891, and by the time he decided to build an estate there in 1919, the ranch had grown to encompass some two hundred fifty thousand acres along fourteen miles of pristine Central California coastline.[1]

The site Hearst chose for his estate was a hilltop 1,600 feet above sea level, with a 360-degree panoramic view of the Pacific Ocean to the west and the steep rolling hills of the Coastal Range to the east. The hilltop had been used by the Hearst family as a camping site since William was a little boy. The only way to get to it was to climb or ride a horse up five

ABOVE: Hearst Castle, San Simeon, view of "La Cuesta Encantada" (The Enchanted Hill). FACING: Hearst Castle, Casa del Mar, House A, view from sitting room into bedroom.

miles of treacherous hillside. The only sign of civilization in sight was a tiny fishing village on the shores of San Simeon Bay and a thousand-foot-long wharf George Hearst had built in 1878.

William Randolph first approached Julia Morgan about designing an estate for him at San Simeon in April of 1919, just after his mother had died during the Great Influenza Epidemic. He visited Morgan in her San Francisco office one night, eager to share with her some ideas he had garnered for this major new project. Walter Steilberg, one of Julia's best draftsmen, recalled this visit years later in an interview he gave for the Bancroft Library:

> I was at my table, after five o'clock—I often worked late because it was interesting work, whatever it was. I heard this voice, which I had heard before, but I didn't realize what a high pitch Mr. Hearst's voice had. For such a large man, it seemed to me his pitch was very high, so it carried.

I heard him say to Miss Morgan, "I would like to build something up on the hill at San Simeon. I get tired of going up there and camping in tents. I'm getting a little too old for that. I'd like to get something that would be a little more comfortable. The other day I was in Los Angeles, prowling around second-hand book stores, as I often do, and I came upon this stack of books called Bungalow Books. Among them I saw this one which has a picture—this isn't what I want, but it gives you an idea of my thought about the thing, keeping it simple, of a Jappo-Swisso bungalow." He laughed at this, and so did she.

Steilberg remembered that Hearst's initial concept quickly evolved into a much larger project: "Well, it quickly became apparent that Mr. Hearst wanted something grand. I don't think it was a month before we were going on the grand scale."[2]

Reading this account might give one the impression that William Randolph Hearst did not have a very clear sense of architectural styles. Indeed, this has been cited by some critics as the reason why, in their opinion, Hearst Castle is a "mishmash," or a "pastiche" of architectural styles, with no clear unifying theme. Yet these are erroneous assumptions, which a close look at the correspondence between Mr. Hearst and Julia Morgan during the planning stages of San Simeon clearly reveals.

Most of the communication between Hearst and Morgan about the plans for San Simeon in late 1919 and early 1920 was done by telegram. In one of his longer letters, cabled to Julia on December 31, 1919, Hearst discusses his stylistic preferences for the overall theme of the buildings that were soon to be built at his new estate:

> I have thought a great deal over whether to make this whole group of buildings Baroc [sic], in the Eighteenth Century Style, or Renaissance. It is quite a problem. I started out with the Baroc idea in mind, as nearly all the Spanish architecture in America is of that character; and the plaster surfaces that we associate all Spanish architecture in California with are a modification of that style, as I understand it.
>
> If we should decide on this style, I would at least want to depart from the very crude and rude example of it that we have in our early California Spanish architecture. This style at its best is sufficiently satisfactory, though in our early California architecture it seems to me too primitive, and in many of the examples I have seen in Mexico so elaborate as to be objectionable.
>
> The alternative is to build this group of buildings in the Renaissance style of Southern Spain. We picked out the towers of the Church of Ronda. I suppose they are Renaissance or else transitional, and they have some Gothic feeling; but a Renaissance decoration, particularly that of the very southern part of Spain, would harmonize well with them. The Renaissance of northern Spain seems to me very hard, while

the Renaissance of southern Spain is much softer and more graceful. We get very beautiful decoration both for the central building and for the cottages out of this Southern Spain Renaissance style, and I think that would, in the main, be the best period for the interior decoration. The trouble would be, I suppose, that it has no historic association with California, or rather with the Spanish architecture in California.

I would very much like to have your views on what we should do in regard to this group of buildings, what style of architecture we should select. I think the Renaissance decoration can be adapted to the smooth plaster surfaces. I think it is so in the church of Ronda and in certain cities in the south of Spain and in the Balaeric Islands. They call it pateresque. Do they not? In writing me your opinion, can you give me some sketches to make the matter more clear?[3]

The tone of this letter also disproves another common misconception about the nature of the working relationship between William Randolph Hearst and Julia Morgan. It has been assumed by many critics, as well as first-time visitors to San Simeon, that Mr. Hearst's huge ego caused him to take a domineering attitude towards both the process of designing all of the buildings and his interactions with Miss Morgan. Yet his constant use of the word "we" in his communications with Morgan, as well as his frequent deferring to her opinion in matters of style and logistics, should serve to dispel such notions. Clearly, the creation of Hearst Castle, from start to finish, was a joint effort between two creative and visionary individuals.

Between 1920, when construction began on the Hearst estate at San Simeon, and 1947, when work ended on the unfinished project, a total of eight major structures were built on the hilltop that William dubbed "La Cuesta Encantada" (The Enchanted Hill). These were: the Main Building, or Casa Grande; three guesthouses, first called A, B, and C, and later named Casa del Mar (House of the Sea), Casa del Monte (House of the Mountain), and Casa del Sol (House of the Sun); the Neptune Pool (or outdoor pool); the Roman Pool (or indoor pool, with a tennis court on its roof); and two attached wings that were added to Casa Grande, the North Wing, and the South Wing. In all, there are 165 rooms, as well as 127 acres of landscaped gardens, fountains, pools, patios, terraces, and walkways.[4] Julia Morgan was involved in designing all of these spaces, always in close consultation with Mr. Hearst. In one telegram she sent to Hearst from her office in San Francisco on December 31, 1919, she reveals her eagerness to begin construction on the project, as well as her practical and sensible approach to the enormous task she had agreed to undertake:

Have mailed you copy of plot plan. Have completed foundation plans for houses B and C. May I start work on these as this would not be

FACING: Hearst Castle, Casa del Mar, House A, 1920–22, looking west. ABOVE: Hearst Castle, Casa del Mar, House A, 1920–22, detail of front entrance.

changed by later decisions on decorative detail of exterior. It will save expense in medium bad weather by utilizing men's time right at site. Am afraid open loggia treatment of lower story House A takes away very much from effectiveness of exterior but will send studies of it for your judgement [*sic*], also studies showing new treatment of cornices etc. as soon as possible.[5]

Julia Morgan faced a number of daunting challenges in carrying out her plans at San Simeon. First, there was the steep, rugged terrain of the site itself, which would quickly have discouraged a less determined architect. A five-mile-long, sharply winding dirt road had to be built to get men, materials, and machinery up to the top of the hillside. Then tons of rock and boulders had to be removed from the hilltop before the foundations could be laid for any of the buildings. It took weeks of blasting with dynamite, and numerous earth-moving machines, to complete this task. There was also the problem of no water supply on the hillside. Morgan solved this problem by constructing a reservoir atop one of the highest peaks on the Hearst Ranch, Pine Mountain, which rises about three thousand feet above sea level. Rain and spring water were then piped down from this peak to "La Cuesta Encatada."[6] All of these jobs put Julia Morgan's skills as an engineer to the test, and her solutions are admired by modern engineers to this day.

Another set of problems was created by the remote location of San Simeon. The wharf that George Hearst had built in the 1870s was not large enough for oceangoing steamships. So Julia Morgan designed a larger pier that could handle the ships carrying building materials and art objects for the new estate. She also designed a Mission Revival warehouse at the foot of the new road to store many of the larger statues and antiques until they could be incorporated into the new buildings on the hilltop.[7]

The men Morgan hired to work on the construction site had to live in tents the first winter, and many complained bitterly about the cold, damp weather and poor cooking and sanitation facilities. So Julia designed a series of houses for several of the more essential workers and contractors and their families at the base of the hill. The number of workers Morgan employed to work at San Simeon fluctuated, from a low of twenty-five to thirty-five in the winter months during slow years, to a high of ninety-five at the peak of the building program in the late 1920s.[8]

Then there was the difficulty of dealing with the financial uncertainties created by Mr. Hearst himself. The budget for this enormous project was never clearly spelled out, and Julia Morgan had to adapt to ever-changing cash flows each month. Hearst gave her a monthly allowance, out of which she was expected to pay all of the expenses, from worker salaries and building materials to her own commission. These amounts ranged from $500 a month at the start of the project to as much $60,000 a month at the height of construction in the late 1920s.[9] Further complicating

FACING: Hearst Castle, Casa del Sol, House C, detail of bedroom ceiling. TOP: Hearst Castle, Casa del Sol, House C, 1920–23. ABOVE: Hearst Castle, view from Casa del Mar towards ocean.

ABOVE: Hearst Castle, Casa del Monte, House B, 1920–23. FACING: Hearst Castle, Casa del Monte, House B, side elevation, 1920. Courtesy of CED, UC Berkeley.

matters was the fact that Hearst rarely paid his bills on time, a habit he had developed as a young newspaper owner and publisher who did not have to answer to anyone else. The fact that Julia managed to keep the construction of San Simeon moving forward under these conditions for twenty-eight years is no small feat.

One personal difficulty that Julia Morgan had to face during this project, which is often overlooked in the books and articles that have been published about San Simeon, was the ordeal of traveling back and forth from San Francisco to the hilltop every week, regardless of weather, and despite her advancing age. When construction began at San Simeon, Julia was forty-eight years old, and she was seventy-five when the project ended.

Carol Paden, daughter of Hearst's general contractor at San Simeon, recalled Morgan's extraordinary vigor on the job in a 1984 interview.

Julia had to hold onto my father's belt when she walked around construction sites because she had Meniere's disease, an imbalance of bones

in her inner ear that caused dizziness and was the result of her childhood ear infections. Yet she never let that slow her down, and would climb up scaffolding constantly—even though she fell and hurt herself badly several times.[10]

Morgan first visited the site in August of 1919 to take stock of all the preliminary work that had to be done. After that, for the next nineteen years, she made the five-hundred-mile round trip from San Francisco to San Simeon every weekend, and then continued to visit the site at least once a month until the continuous construction phase ceased in 1942. The trip took much longer then and involved a seven-hour train ride to San Luis Obispo, and then a forty-five-mile taxi ride to the hilltop. Although Julia was never one to complain about any of the difficult working conditions she endured during her career, she did comment in a letter to Hearst in 1921 about the road trip from the San Luis Obispo train station through two small towns to San Simeon. She wrote, "If you would like to break every bone in your worst enemy's body treat him to the road trip from Cayucos to Cambria."[11]

Julia Morgan did all this traveling, and supervised construction of the San Simeon estate, while she was designing and building an average of eighteen structures a year all around the states of California and Hawaii. Few architects today, even the most successful and prolific ones, could ever hope to match this remarkable record of achievement.

The preliminary work to prepare the site at San Simeon was carried out during the late summer and autumn of 1919. Construction finally began on the three guesthouses in February of 1920. Hearst had agreed to delay the start of construction on "Casa Grande" until after the guesthouses were completed, as Julia Morgan had suggested in her letters to him during the planning phase of the project.

The three "bungalows," as the guesthouses were often referred to, were arranged around the western edge of a curved walkway that was named the Esplanade. This paved walkway encircled a terraced, lushly landscaped piazza, which stood in front of the site for the Main Building, or Casa Grande. House A, or Casa Del Mar, was at the southern end of the group and faced southwest to take advantage of the unspoiled views of the coastline and the Pacific Ocean. This was planned as Hearst's first residence at San Simeon. House C, or Casa del Sol, was actually set in the middle of the walkway, and faced due west to capture the best views of the sunset. House B, or Casa del Monte, was at the north end of the group and was sited slightly lower on the hillside than the other two. It faced due north so that it would provide a magnificent view of the Santa Lucia Mountain Range.

Construction on all three of the guesthouses was largely complete by the summer of 1923. They would have been finished much earlier, but Hearst kept demanding changes to both the exterior and interior of the "bungalows" while construction was underway. The most extensive change that was made was to House C, Casa del Sol, where Hearst decided, after it was nearly finished in 1921, to build two towers above the bathrooms to bring the roofline up to the level of the other two bungalows.[12]

To call these guesthouses bungalows is more than a little misleading. They were much larger, and had more levels, than the traditional one-story bungalows with low, sloping rooflines so popular with middle-class home builders of that period. Casa del Mar has 3,500 square feet of living space on three levels with eighteen rooms, including eight bedrooms, six baths, three lobbies, a sitting room, and a loggia. This was Hearst's living quarters until Casa Grande was sufficiently finished for him to move into by the end of 1925. Casa del Sol also has eighteen rooms on three levels with over three thousand square feet of living space, including eight bedrooms and a large sitting room. Casa del Monte has ten rooms on two levels, including four bedrooms, four bathrooms, a sitting room, and a lobby.[13]

Stylistically, all three of the guesthouses were designed in the southern Spanish Renaissance style that was the unifying theme for all the residences at San Simeon. The main entrances to the bungalows are on the single level that faces the Esplanade, while the rear of each house has multiple levels facing outward from the steep slopes of the hillside. Casa del Mar has an imposing rear facade, with a Renaissance balustraded double staircase rising towards the central two-story tower. The tower has three arched windows on the lower level, and rectangular banded windows on the second level, which provide guests with maximum views of the Pacific Ocean. Casa del Sol has an ornate three-story rear facade, with a Spanish Renaissance loggia on the top level flanked by balconies, and banded picture-glass windows across the upper story. There is a curved double staircase leading to the rear entrance and a superb sixteenth-century Spanish fountain in the courtyard with a replica of Donatello's "David" perched atop it. Casa del Sol has a hipped roof with twin Moorish towers at each end, which are embellished with Moorish-style wooden balcony screens. The front of this house is decorated with intricate Moorish tiles and metalwork. Casa del Monte is not as visible from the rear as the other two bungalows. It has a simple double staircase leading up to the two-story rear facade, with banded windows and Spanish Renaissance balconies across the upper level.

For many first-time visitors to Hearst Castle, the highlight of their tour is the Neptune Pool. This large outdoor swimming pool is at the southwestern corner of La Cuesta Encantada, below the guest-houses. It was constructed in several stages between 1924 and 1936. The appearance of the Neptune Pool was altered several times during those years, as Hearst continually suggested making it grander and incorporating various ancient artifacts and recent sculptures from his private collection.

By the early 1930s, the Neptune Pool had reached its current length of 104 feet, with a basin that could hold 345,000 gallons of water. It was engineered like no other private pool in California before it. The pool was supported by a complex system, which involved hanging it from reinforced concrete beams that were set into a concrete retaining wall. This system would allow the pool to sway during an earthquake without breaking apart. Above the pool, there is a terrace that has seventeen dressing rooms housed within its foundations. Each dressing room has a full bathroom and full-length mirror.[14]

The aesthetic effect of the Neptune Pool is simply breathtaking. The pool itself has a bottom decorated with black-and-white inlaid marble done in Greco-Roman geometric patterns. Curving around the ends of the oval-shaped basin are twin peristyles, or covered rows of paired columns, which embrace the pool like two elegant arms of marble. These columns are in the Classical Ionic style, enhancing the graceful feeling of the space they embrace.

Dominating the western edge of the pool is the so-called "Roman Temple." This is really a composite structure, created by Julia Morgan by incorporating parts from several ancient Roman temples dating from the first to the fourth century A.D. The marble columns and capitals, pediment, and sections of the frieze were made from fragments of old Roman temples, with modern concrete added to extend and support them. The pediment group was created by Morgan by setting ancient statues of Neptune and the Nereids (or sea nymphs) into concrete.[15]

At the opposite edge of the pool, Julia designed a marble-walled space to display a sculptural group called "The Birth of Venus." This group was designed by the prominent French sculptor Charles Cassou, and Morgan traveled to Paris to personally commission this work from him.

FACING, ABOVE: Hearst Castle, Casa Grande, 1922–27, detail of pediment, with carved figures by Jules Suppo. FACING, BELOW: Hearst Castle, statue, left side of Casa Grande. ABOVE: Hearst Castle, stairs above Neptune Pool, c. 1926.

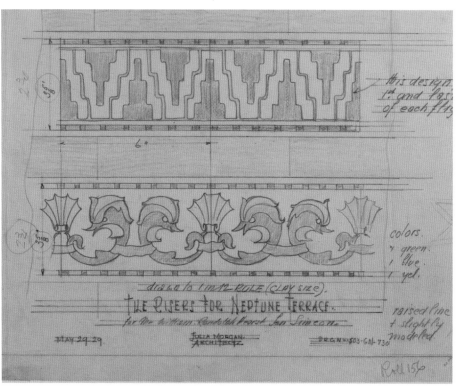

It was set into place in 1934, by which time the Neptune Pool had already been used for several years by Hollywood's elite as a place to relax and enjoy the spectacular views. Photos and home movies taken at Hearst Castle during the 1930s show the likes of Greta Garbo, Buster Keaton, Cary Grant, Jimmy Stewart, and Charlie Chaplin sitting around the pool sipping drinks, chatting, or marveling at the glorious sunsets over the Pacific Ocean from 1,600 feet above sea level.

The other pool at San Simeon is the Roman Pool, often called the "Indoor Pool." The Roman Pool is located at the northeast corner of La Cuesta Encantada, behind Casa Grande. It sits below the tennis courts, which were constructed in 1925 (the courts form the roof of the pool). Hearst asked Julia Morgan to design an indoor pool in 1927, which required the excavation of some of the earth around the tennis courts so that this new pool would be aboveground. Construction on the pool itself did not begin until 1930, and the final tiles were not laid until 1935.

FACING, ABOVE: Hearst Castle, Neptune Pool, with Roman Temple at far end, 1924–36. Photo by Mark A. Wilson. FACING, BELOW: Hearst Castle, Drawing of Terrace above Neptune Pool, c. 1924, completed 1934. Courtesy of CED, UC Berkeley. ABOVE: Hearst Castle, Neptune Pool, with peristyle above, 1924–36. Photo by Mark A. Wilson.

The magnificent visual richness of the Roman Pool was inspired by fourth-century Roman mosaics that Hearst had seen at Ravenna, Italy, during his travels. The pool is in the shape of a "T," with a short stem, or alcove. The depth of the alcove is three and a half feet, while that of the main basin is ten feet. The glorious tile work that covers the entire surface of the Roman Pool was done in a pattern of Murano glass tiles in rich blue, blue green, and twenty-two-carat gold.[16] The borders and some of the rectangular panels were decorated with fish, seahorses, and mermaids. It took three years for the tile setters to finish their work, since Julia Morgan insisted on having every tile set perfectly while giving them a patina of age. Here again, her dedication to perfection paid off, as anyone can attest who has gazed down the length of the Roman Pool and seen the breathtaking beauty of the tiles reflected in its surface.

The construction of Casa Grande got underway in April of 1922. During the next three and a half years, Hearst insisted on numerous changes to this "Main Building," both on the

FACING, ABOVE: Hearst Castle, Roman Pool, 1930–35. FACING, BELOW: Hearst Castle, Roman Pool, 1930–35, diving platform. ABOVE: Hearst Castle, Roman Pool, detail of mosaic tile work.

room design and floor plan of the interior, and on the decoration and scale of the exterior. The entire structure was built of reinforced poured concrete to make the building resistant to earthquakes and fires. The process of pouring the walls of the Main Building took more than two years to complete, and the twin "bell towers" were not completed in their present form until late 1927 (the bells installed near the top of both towers were rung often during Hearst's time, and have been rung on special occasions since then). The interior of the Main Building was complete enough by December 1925 for Hearst to host his first formal Christmas dinner for dozens of guests in the mammoth Assembly Room on the ground floor.[17]

A common misconception about Hearst Castle is that William Randolph Hearst built this immense estate as some sort of "love palace" for his mistress, the actress Marion Davies. The Orson Welles film *Citizen Kane* has perpetuated this myth, along with many other myths about Hearst's life. In truth, when Hearst began building San Simeon, he intended it for his family: his wife, Millicent, and their five sons. Millicent and the Hearst sons began staying in the guesthouses in 1923, and they spent part of the summer of 1924 in the just-completed "cloister bedrooms" in the central section of the second floor of Casa Grande. But by 1925, the Hearsts' marriage had deteriorated to the point of becoming an informal separation. Though they never divorced, William began spending all of his time at Hearst Castle with Marion Davies, although Millicent and his sons still visited from time to time over the years. From the mid-1920s until his last visit to "La Cuesta Encantada" in 1947, William divided most of his time between a suite at the Ambassador Hotel in Los Angeles and San Simeon.[18]

The western facade of Casa Grande is familiar to millions of people all over the United States and around the world. In addition to more than twenty-five million people who have visited Hearst Castle since it opened as a state park in 1958, millions more have seen its likeness in books, magazines, newspaper articles, travel brochures, and TV programs. Part of its appeal is the pleasing Renaissance symmetry of the facade, with its flanking bell towers framing a central gable. The sheer scale of the western facade impresses visitors as well. The towers are 160 feet tall, and the peak of the main gable is 105 feet above the ground.

The Spanish Renaissance details on the west front of Casa Grande, while certainly ornate, do not overwhelm the building. Indeed, contrary to popular assumptions, Morgan left a majority of the facade unornamented. The massive front door is covered by a metal grillwork screen, and it is bordered by lacy bas-relief decorations in late Gothic and early

FACING: Hearst Castle, Casa Grande, close-up of south bell tower. TOP: Hearst Castle, Casa Grande, 1922–27, west front. ABOVE: Hearst Castle, Casa Grande, close-up of front doorway.

ABOVE: Hearst Castle, Casa Grande, Gothic Study, completed 1931. FACING: Hearst Castle, Casa Grande, Assembly Room.

Renaissance style (this blend of styles is what one finds on many fifteenth- and sixteenth-century cathedrals in southern Spain). There are twin statues of knights on pedestals flanking the front door, and a statue of Mary and Jesus stands in a recessed niche above the doorway.

The second level of Casa Grande's facade has two balconies. The lower one is faced with ornately carved stone and runs across the wide central pavilion that projects several feet outward on the first and second levels. The upper balcony is made of wrought iron, with three curved platforms in front of Hearst's private suite, which provided perfect views of his arriving guests as they stepped out of their limousines or taxis in the Central Plaza below. Just above this balcony is one of Casa Grande's

most distinguishing features: a massive wooden cornice with a low-peaked gable in the center. This ornate cornice was carved by Morgan's master woodworker, Jules Suppo, in 1922 and 1923, in his workshop in San Francisco. Suppo decorated the brackets of the teakwood cornice with carved bears, elephants, fish, and other animals. Morgan's use of a central wooden cornice on a masonry facade was inspired by the large pediment on top of the main facade of the Santa Barbara Mission church.

The towers of Casa Grande have three levels. Their bases are octagonal and are unadorned except for the geometric patterns of the cast-concrete window screens. The second level is also octagonal, and houses bells set into paired arched windows. These windows are separated by Renaissance

spiraled columns and framed with beautiful blue and yellow tiles in floral patterns. The towers are capped by round domed cupolas that are ornamented with paired columns topped by carved stone faces, and surfaced in blue-and-yellow tile work in geometric and swag patterns.

The interior of Casa Grande has four levels arranged around a T-shaped floor plan. The total number of rooms in the Main Building equals 115, divided into twenty-six bedrooms, thirty-two bathrooms, fourteen sitting rooms, two libraries, two dining rooms, a movie theater, a billiard room, a kitchen, a pantry, twelve multipurpose rooms, twelve servants' bedrooms, and ten servants' bathrooms. The total square footage of the living area of the Main Building is 54,000, as well as a 14,000 square-foot basement, which contained storage for much of Hearst's collection of art objects and a wine cellar.[19]

The most architecturally interesting rooms in Casa Grande are the Assembly Room, the Refectory, the Morning Room, the Billiard Room,

FACING, ABOVE: Hearst Castle, Casa Grande, Refectory. FACING, BELOW: Hearst Castle, Casa Grande, Refectory, detail of ceiling. ABOVE: Hearst Castle, Casa Grande, Billiard Room.

the Theater, the Doge's Suite, the Library, the Gothic Study, the Gothic Sitting Room, and the North and South Celestial Bedrooms. The Assembly Room is the first space guests enter on the ground floor, and its mammoth proportions made it ideally suited as a reception room for Mr. Hearst's numerous visitors. It is eighty-two feet long, thirty feet wide, and has a twenty-four-foot-high ceiling. The main feature of the Assembly Room is a sixteenth-century French Renaissance stone fireplace mantel set into the wall, which was brought from a chateau in Burgundy. This room was not completely finished until 1928.[20]

The Refectory, or Dining Hall, runs east from the Assembly Room. This is where all of the formal meals were served at San Simeon. It is over eighty feet long and nearly twenty-five feet wide, and has a twenty-seven-foot-high ceiling, the tallest at San Simeon. The overall ambience of this room is Gothic, in contrast to the Renaissance style of many other rooms in Casa Grande. The walls are lined with a fourteenth-century Gothic wooden choir stall from Spain, and there is a Gothic-style carved stone fireplace at one end. The ceiling, however, is decorated with fifteen French Renaissance high-relief coffered panels in wood, which depict life-sized figures of saints, coats-of-arms, and the Virgin Mary. Hearst was not a religious man, but Julia Morgan incorporated this antique ceiling into the Refectory because it was the only one he had purchased that would fit the space.[21]

FACING: Hearst Castle, Casa Grande, Main Library. ABOVE: Hearst Castle, Casa Grande, South Celestial Bedroom, completed 1926.

ABOVE: Hearst Castle, Casa Grande, Doge's Suite, completed 1926. FACING, ABOVE: Hearst Castle, Casa Grande, Doge's Suite, window detail. FACING, BELOW: Hearst Castle, Casa Grande, Doge's Suite, bedroom.

The Morning Room is a large sitting room just east of the Refectory. This room also has a Gothic feel, with its massive beamed ceiling, thirteenth-century marble archway from a Spanish cathedral, and Gothic stone mantelpiece from a medieval French chateau. There are four seventeenth-century Flemish tapestries hanging on the walls of this room.

To the north of the Morning Room is the Billiard Room, which is part of the North Wing, an addition to the Main Building that was begun in 1929. This room has a fifteenth-century Spanish-painted beamed ceiling, a French Renaissance stone fireplace mantel, and a French Gothic tapestry of a "Hunting Scene." At the northeast corner of the ground floor, adjacent to the Billiard Room, is the Theater, where Hearst showed feature films every night to any guests or employees who wanted to watch them. The only ornamental features here are the gilded caryatids, or female figures, used as columns. These Baroque-looking caryatids are holding lamps in their hands and they are similar to the ones Julia Morgan had designed for the interior of the Women's Building at the Panama-Pacific Exposition in San Francisco in 1915.[22]

The Library is at the west end of the second floor, and it is located above the Assembly Room. The most striking feature of the Library is the sixteenth-century Spanish Renaissance coffered ceiling. The walls are lined with bookshelves designed by Julia Morgan, which are framed by Corinthian pilasters. This room contains four thousand books, as well as some of Hearst's superb collection of ancient Greek vases. There is a massive neoclassical marble fireplace set into one wall, which is a fifteenth-century Italian antique. To the west of the Library is a large Lobby, which has Spanish Renaissance–style bas-relief wooden panels, most of which were designed by Morgan. The Lobby also incorporates parts of the same sixteenth-century Spanish ceiling that was used in the Library.

At the rear of the second story, Morgan designed a mezzanine section called the Doge's Suite. Completed in 1926, this was the first section of the Main Building to be occupied. Hearst had only his most important guests assigned to sleep in the Doge's Suite, which was enlarged in 1931 when the North and South Wings were constructed, in order to preserve the fine view of the flower-bordered rear courtyard and the hills to the east. The Doge's Suite includes a sitting room, a north and south bedroom, a balcony, the lower north duplex, the lower south duplex, and a porch. The sitting room incorporated a painted Dutch ceiling, which had once been installed in the upstate New York home of the famous architect Stanford White. The most interesting section of the Doge's Suite is the exquisite Venetian Gothic loggia that Julia

ABOVE: Hearst Castle, Casa Grande, detail of window on east facade. BELOW: Hearst Castle, rear view of Casa Grande.

Morgan designed for the balcony. Hearst had originally planned to have the rear courtyard covered with a domed Great Hall, which Morgan drew up a set of plans for that were never used.[23]

The Gothic Study was designed to be Hearst's office and private library when he was at San Simeon. It is located on the third floor, two stories above the Refectory. The Gothic Study was constructed in 1931, and it was the last major room to be finished in Casa Grande. The creation of this room presented Julia Morgan with some serious design challenges, since the space Hearst had designated for it originally had a low ceiling with very little wall space for windows, making it feel dark and cramped. Her solution was simple, yet brilliant. She proposed raising the roof over this section of Casa Grande, thus creating a higher ceiling that would be supported by steel beams disguised as a series of sweeping Gothic arches made of concrete. This

reconfiguring of the roofline also allowed space for a clerestory of Gothic-arched windows, which were tinted pink to bathe the room in a soft glowing light. Julia had to lobby Hearst repeatedly to get him to accept the added expense of this remodeling.[24]

The aesthetic effect of the Gothic Study is truly stunning. The row of Gothic arches spans the width of the room from floor to ceiling, creating a powerful visual rhythm. The flat surfaces of these arches were decorated with colorful frescoes of figures from the Bible and medieval life, which were painted by one of Morgan's best artists, Camille Solon.[25] A fifteenth-century Spanish beamed ceiling was installed between these arches. Bookshelves line the walls of the study, which contains four thousand of Hearst's most valuable books. A heroic portrait of a young William Randolph Hearst, painted in 1893 by his longtime friend Orrin Peck, stares out commandingly from the west end of the room. The rich earth tones of the wood paneling, frescoes, parquet floor, and beamed ceiling in the Gothic Study create a feeling of medieval opulence.

The North and South Celestial Bedrooms are the crowing architectural jewels of Hearst Castle. They are located on the fourth level of Casa Grande, in the bell towers just below the belfries. They were created in 1926 when the bell towers were raised about twenty feet, and two bedroom suites were created within the extra space this provided. Each of the Celestial Suites consists of a large octagonal bedroom with a bathroom and small closet on the landing below. The bedrooms have to be approached via a narrow, winding turret staircase.

ABOVE: Hearst Castle, Casa Grande, view of North Wing, added 1931. BELOW: Hearst Castle, boneyard of unused sculpture behind Casa Grande.

The inconvenience of not having a place to hang one's clothes within the bedrooms is far outweighed by the heavenly beauty of the rooms themselves. The ceilings consist of gilded beams framing deep, coffered panels lined with delicate frescoes depicting birds of paradise. The walls are hung with twenty-foot-tall gold brocade drapes, and the six-foot-tall windows in each room are ornamented with gold-painted open-work tracery in Arabesque patterns. There is a glass door set into each bedroom, which allows guests to enjoy the superb views of "La Cuesta Encantada" and the unspoiled Pacific coastline below. It is no wonder that such famous guests as the gossip columnist Hedda Hopper and the children's book author Ludwig Bemelmans were quite happy to sleep in either one of these aptly named Celestial Suites.

William Randolph Hearst and Marion Davies playing croquet at Wyntoon, c. 1930s. Courtesy of Mrs. Jean Henry Willcombe.

The other country estate that Julia Morgan designed for William Randolph Hearst, one which few people have heard of and even fewer have seen, is called Wyntoon. Hidden among the tall pine trees along a double bend of the McCloud River in Shasta County, about fifty miles south of the Oregon border, Wyntoon is a family compound that is not listed on California maps (the name was taken from the Indian word for this area). Located about twenty miles north of Lake Shasta and fifteen miles south of Mount Shasta, Wyntoon is still privately owned by the Hearst Family, and is not open to the public.

The setting of Wyntoon conjures up images of the foothills of the Bavarian Alps. The clear waters of the McCloud River are quite turbulent as they rush between the dense growth of old pine trees, some of which tower more than a hundred feet above the riverbanks. The site is about 3,300 feet above sea level. The rugged peaks of the Cascade Mountains rise in the distance, the most famous of which is Mount Shasta, with an elevation of over 14,000 feet. The crisp, clean mountain air and the seclusion of the setting make this an ideal place to escape the pressures of city life and reinvigorate one's mind and body.

The Hearst Family estate at Wyntoon began around 1900, when Phoebe Hearst got her lawyer to lease a plot of land next to his country house on the McCloud River, which had been designed by noted San Francisco architect Willis Polk. Phoebe then hired Bernard Maybeck to design for her a seven-story-tall, German Gothic–style "Castle," which was completed in 1902. She eventually purchased her lawyer's land and acquired a fifty-thousand-acre estate.[26] After Phoebe died, William continued to visit Wyntoon often, enjoying the beauty and isolation of this pristine setting, where he had spent so many happy hours during his youth.

Then, in 1930, Maybeck's Castle burned to the ground in a kitchen fire. Hearst decided to hire both Maybeck and Julia Morgan to design a new "Castle" on the site of the old one. Maybeck and Morgan drew up plans for a huge Bavarian Gothic–style, eight-story castle that would have two massive towers, numerous turrets, and sixty-one bedrooms. While Mr. Hearst was enamored of this plan, he soon realized that he could not afford the enormous expense of such a project just as the Great Depression was deepening and while he was still involved in finishing work on Casa Grande at San Simeon. He decided to abandon this grandiose plan, and hired Julia Morgan to design for him a more modest "Bavarian Village" on his estate at Wyntoon. Hearst paid to have Morgan flown in his private plane to Bavaria to sketch medieval buildings that might serve as models for his new Bavarian Village.[27]

Julia Morgan's plan for Wyntoon makes marvelous use of the natural features of the site, in the manner of her best First Bay Tradition designs. Although the style of most of her buildings at Wyntoon can be described roughly as Medieval German or Austrian, each structure integrates with the environment in a way that is quite site-sensitive, both in its use of local materials and in its specific placement and purpose in relation to the riverbank itself.

Morgan designed a total of sixteen structures at the Wyntoon estate. These included several buildings constructed before she created the new master plan: a superintendent's house (1924); servants' quarters (1924); stables with a caretaker's house (1925); and "The Chalet" (i.e., upscale servants' quarters resembling a Swiss Chalet, 1925). The first

ABOVE: The driveway at the Bavarian Village, Wyntoon, completed 1933, with the Cinderella House in the foreground, and the Fairy House in back. Photo by Lynn McMurray. BELOW: Wyntoon, River House, side elevation, remodel by Julia Morgan, 1935. Courtesy of CED, UC Berkeley.

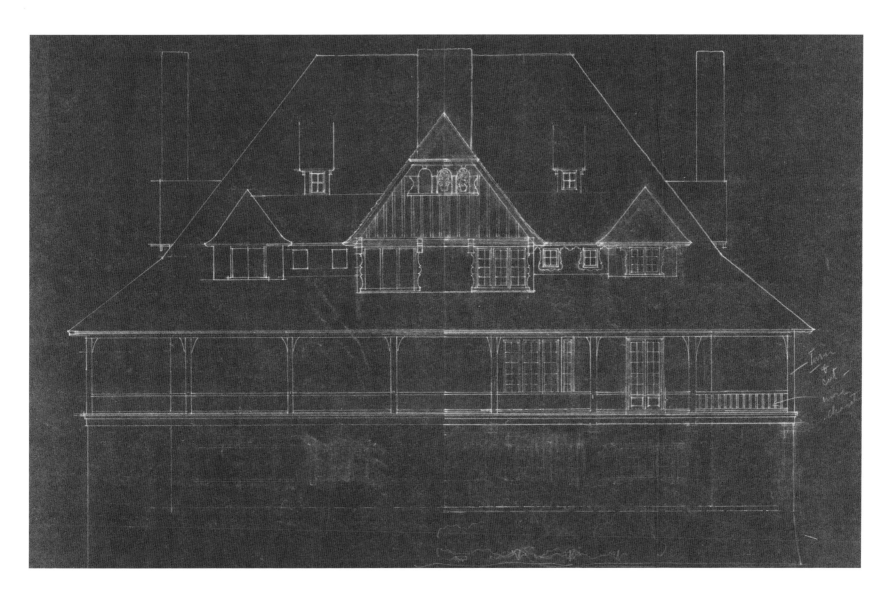

TOP: The Bend, Wyntoon, built 1935–41 (stone building still standing, house on right burned down). Photo by Lynn McMurray. ABOVE: Detail of fresco on Cinderella House by Willy Pogany, from the Russian fairy tale "The Three Ugly Sisters." Photo c. 1930s by Mr. H. Forney.

three structures that she designed in the 1932 master plan were guesthouses completed in 1933, and they were given romantic names befitting their picturesque appearances: Cinderella House, Fairy House, and Bear House.

Each house is three stories tall, with half-timbered exteriors, steeply pitched gables, and German Gothic–style wood decoration both inside and out, much of it carved by Jules Suppo or his assistants. Some of the exterior paintings, such as decorative patterns on the shutters, were done by Doris Day, who had worked with Julia on the Chapel of the Chimes in Oakland. But the most distinctive feature of the guesthouses was the charming, Disney-like frescoes painted on the exteriors of the Cinderella and Bear Houses by noted muralist Willy Pogany. These colorful frescoes depict scenes from various Russian and Brothers Grimm fairy tales, and were recently restored to the original luster by Pogany's son.[28]

Julia Morgan sited these three guesthouses along a front driveway that curves around a green lawn shaded by tall pines. The rear facades of the houses are aligned with a bend of the McCloud River, and they have multiple balconies and dormer windows to allow guests to enjoy unfettered views of the racing waters below and primeval forests all around. The natural textures and careful placement of these romantic hideaways make them harmonize perfectly with their Alpine-like setting.

The other buildings Julia Morgan designed as part of her master plan for Hearst's estate at Wyntoon were: the Bridge House (1933); the pool and pool houses (1934–35); offices (1935); the River House (remodeled by her in 1935); the Teahouse (1935); the Bend (1935–41); and the Gables (1937). Of these, all remain intact today except for the Gables, the interior of which was gutted by an accidental fire in 1945.

The Bridge House stands directly across the river from the River House. It is an impressive, five-story, Medieval Teutonic tower reminiscent of the fortified German toll towers along the Rhine River. Morgan had the exterior clad in wood shingles, which both softens its effect and makes it blend in with the surrounding forest. The interior of the Bridge

RIGHT: Bear House, Wyntoon, front view. Photo by Lynn McMurray. BELOW: Wyntoon, Oriel (Bear) House, front elevation, 1932. Courtesy of CED, UC Berkeley.

House incorporated a movie theater where Hearst had nightly showings of films for his guests. Morgan also remodeled the earlier River House (designed by Willis Polk) to serve as an extra guesthouse. She included a small Art Deco marble pool beside the main house for guest use. Her remodel also enhanced the view of the river visitors had from the windows facing the veranda.[29]

Just south of the Bridge House along the banks of the McCloud River stands the Teahouse. Morgan designed this as a multipurpose entertainment facility, with a pavilion for dances, a boat dock, and areas for drinking tea and having picnics. The exterior of the Teahouse displays a simpler version of the German medieval style Julia had used for the three main guesthouses, with rusticated stone walls and a Gothic archway facing the river on the lower level, half-timbering across the upper level, and a steeply pitched hipped roof rising to a pointed metal spire.

The Bend is about a half-mile south of the Teahouse, facing a sharp curve in the river. This is a connected group of buildings that were added by Julia Morgan onto the original Willis Polk–designed house between

ABOVE: The Fairy House, Wyntoon. Photo by Lynn McMurray. BELOW: Groundbreaking ceremony for the original Wyntoon, c. 1901. Photo courtesy of Lynn McMurray.

1935 and 1941. In the middle are two solid fieldstone structures that resemble small English medieval halls, with their pointed arched windows lined with tracery and a wall with crenellated battlements rising behind them. At the east end of the compound, Morgan designed a superb half-timbered, German medieval two-story house with twin high-peaked gables and an overhang on the second story and fieldstone walls and three recessed doorways on the first story (this house burned down in an accidental fire). The interior of the Bend includes a large dining hall and living quarters.

Just as at San Simeon, work on the Wyntoon estate was never completely finished. Yet at both of these sites, Julia Morgan had created ideal, self-contained romantic worlds. San Simeon and Wyntoon present images of remarkable beauty, which incorporate the materials and vistas of their magnificent natural settings, while exhibiting the exquisite craftsmanship and attention to detail that are the hallmark of their exceptional architect.

RIGHT: Bear House, rear view, Wyntoon. Photo by Lynn McMurray. BELOW, LEFT: Cinderella House, rear view, Wyntoon. Photo by Lynn McMurray. BELOW, RIGHT: Cinderella House, front view, Wyntoon. Photo by H. Forney.

CHAPTER II

Private Spaces

Rosenburg was known as "The Dried Fruit King of Fresno" before he moved to San Francisco, and the residence Morgan designed for him is of truly baronial proportions.

—Abraham Rosenburg House, 1917

I t was in her single-family residences that Julia Morgan's incredible versatility, her amazing productivity, and her sensitivity to clients' needs was most clearly demonstrated. During her forty-four years of active residential work, Morgan designed and completed over five hundred houses in dozens of communities throughout California. These range from simple wooden bungalows in the Craftsman or First Bay Tradition mode to grand mansions in Georgian, Tudor, or Italian Renaissance Revival style. In every one of these homes, no matter what budget she had to work with, she applied her dedication to craftsmanship and attention to detail that made her residences so pleasing to her clients.

In 1902, just after her return from the Ecole des Beaux-Arts in Paris, Julia Morgan designed two houses, one for Frederick and Mabel Seares on the University of Missouri campus in Columbia, Missouri, and a cottage for Mary Smith in the Arbor Villa section of Oakland. Both of these homes were demolished long ago.[1] Morgan's residential work began in earnest in 1904, after she opened her own office in San Francisco.

Berkeley was where Julia began her education as an architect, and it was in this city that she received some of her earliest residential commissions. The earliest remaining example of Morgan's residential work in Berkeley is the home she designed for Annie Edmonds at 2612 Regent Street in 1904. The Edmonds House is a two-and-a-half-story Craftsman residence, with a brown-shingle exterior, a clinker brick chimney, and latticed windows. The low-angled overhanging gables have bargeboards and exposed roof beams. Two small wooden balconies, one on the third level and one on the second story, provided residents with marvelous views of the East Bay hills and the bay. This is a simple yet elegant example of Morgan's philosophy of nature-based design in her early residential commissions.[2]

Some of the first homes Julia Morgan created in Berkeley were speculative houses, such as the pair of nearly identical two-story residences

FACING: Mr. Abraham Rosenburg House, San Francisco, 1917, view of dining room towards patio. ABOVE: Annie Edmonds House, Berkeley, 1904. Courtesy of Lynn McMurray.

she designed in 1906 for Louise Goddard at 2531 and 2535 Etna Street.[3] These simple brown-shingle homes straddle a common driveway and have no decorative details on their exteriors. However, with their sophisticated placement of banded latticed windows, low gables with wide, overhanging eaves, natural materials, and street scale to integrate with their site, they display all of the basic elements of the First Bay Tradition. These two speculative houses, and three others Morgan designed for Goddard in 1905 at 2615, 2617, and 2619 Parker Street, met the needs of her client by providing her with high-quality houses to sell to future home buyers.

ABOVE: Speculative House, Berkeley, 2816 Derby Street, 1908. BELOW: Speculative houses for Louise Goddard, 2531 and 2535 Etna Street, Berkeley, 1906.

In 1908, Morgan designed two speculative houses at 2816 and 2814 Derby Street, which were lived in by members of her staff, including the draftsman Thaddeus Joy, who later bought number 2816.[4] These brown-shingle homes have side entrances off a shared brick driveway. They both have two stories, with low-angled gables and arched windows in their attics, but otherwise they are quite different. Number 2816 has ornate neoclassical balusters framing a marvelous Palladian window on the upper story. The front door is flanked by tapered, shingled buttresses, with a shingled pediment above. Number 2814 has triple-lighted windows on the upper story, and an angled bay with five banded windows and delightful Celtic carved wood patterns on the first floor. The arched doorway has latticed sidelights and is covered by a deep awning supported by shingled Doric columns.

One of the first major residential commissions Julia Morgan completed was the three-story house she designed in 1905 for Professor William Colby at 2901 Channing Way, near the UC Berkeley campus. This massive eight-bedroom residence commands a steep corner lot and takes full advantage of its site by providing marvelous views of San Francisco Bay and the Golden Gate Bridge. Its brown-shingle exterior, banded plate-glass windows, and horizontal massing that makes it seem a part of the landscape, mark the Colby House as an early example of Morgan's First Bay Tradition work. In the 1980s, the residence was converted into a novitiate house for Dominican nuns. It now serves as the Sigma Phi Epsilon Fraternity House for the UC campus.

Just above the UC Berkeley Football Stadium, at 5–11 Panoramic Way, Morgan created a sophisticated neo-Tudor-style apartment building for Professor Clifton Price in 1910. This three-story residential income building has a stucco facade, high-peaked gables, half-timbering on the upper level, and a second-story overhang. There is a raised deck in front of the entrance, which has an arched, recessed doorway. Three bay windows project from the second story, and Morgan placed banded windows along the ground floor.

Marin Avenue in North Berkeley runs from near the bay to the top of the Berkeley Hills, at Grizzly Peak Boulevard. Morgan designed two very different residences on Marin Avenue. The first one was the Ralph White House in 1913, at 1841 Marin. At first glance, this appears to be a small Craftsman bungalow. But after closer examination, one notices that it is much larger and more subtly elegant than most bungalows. What looks like a low-sloping roofline from the front is actually a tall high-peaked gable when viewed from the side. The upper story

is much more spacious than the usual partial second story on other bungalows.

But it is Morgan's refined fenestration that distinguishes the Ralph White House as a fine example of the First Bay Tradition. The central bay window has delicate neoclassical proportions and decorative trim. Flanking this are triple-lighted latticed windows on each end of the first floor that wrap around the southwest corner to admit maximum natural light into the home's interior. And the front door is sheltered by a small recessed porch behind the latticed windows on the northeast corner of the house, which serves to protect anyone entering the home from the cold, rainy weather in winter.

A few blocks further east, where Marin Avenue becomes one of the steepest streets in the Bay Area, Julia Morgan designed a home at number 2118 for George Bell in 1914. This two-story stucco and wood-trim house is a unique essay in the Swiss chalet mode. The north side of the house faces Marin Avenue and is set back well from the street behind a high wooden fence, allowing its residents to enjoy the marvelous bay view from the west-facing front in complete privacy (the enclosed sun porch was added by Morgan in 1922). Diamond-paned casement windows lined with flower boxes, wide overhanging eaves, half-timber trim, and carved geometric patterns on the shutters give the Bell House an air of authentic Alpine craftsmanship.

Further north in the Berkeley Hills, at 834 Santa Barbara Road, Julia Morgan designed an Arts and Crafts gem for two women doctors in 1915. Dr. E. L. Mitchell and Dr. M. L. Williams chose a steep lot with a fine Golden Gate view for their four-bedroom, two-bath house. Morgan's solution to the challenge of building a home with adequate living space

ABOVE: Speculative House, Berkeley 2814 Derby Street, 1908. BELOW: Ralph White House, Berkeley, 1913.

on such a steep, narrow site was ideal. The house has a street-level entry, with a spacious living room and an adjacent dining room and a long kitchen, all on the upper level. A staircase leads to the living quarters on the lower level, with two large bedrooms along the south side of the lower level, and a full bath in between. There are two more modest bedrooms and a full bath along the west end. In the northeast corner, below the one-car garage, is an office. A partial basement includes a study and built-in shelving for storage. Thus, Morgan's design literally hugs the hillside as it uses the steep slope to perfect advantage.

From the sidewalk, the Mitchell-Williams House appears to be a small, simple, brown-shingle cottage with a hipped roof and an attached garage, the only ornament being Celtic patterns made of wrought iron set into narrow windows in the entryway. But once inside, the soaring,

ABOVE: Wallace McGregor House, Berkeley, 1920. BELOW: George Bell House, Berkeley, 1914.

open-beamed redwood ceiling creates a surprising feeling of openness. An original Arts and Crafts copper lamp hangs from the center beam. Banded casement windows along the south wall and paired casement windows flanking a fireplace on the west wall give the living room a light, airy quality. The dining room has the same light and open feeling, with its banded windows facing San Francisco Bay. The ambience that Morgan created here is one of beauty, comfort, and warmth.

The Thousand Oaks district in the North Berkeley Hills was graced with two of Julia Morgan's most distinctive residences. Geographically, this area is distinguished by the presence of large outcroppings of exposed bedrock, which dominate many of the lots and present special challenges to anyone building a home on such a site. Morgan handled this challenge beautifully with her design for the Ralph Eltse House, built in 1915 at 1937 Thousand Oaks Boulevard. The most noteworthy feature of this residence is the way it embraces the large rock formation at the top of its sloping, tree-shaded lot. The facade of this two-story house seems to wrap around the rocks, with a modified U-shaped floor plan.

The exterior of the Eltse House has a blend of Arts and Crafts and Mediterranean features. The roof is made of red clay tiles and the walls are of pastel stucco, with round-arched windows underlined by flower boxes. At the south end of the house is a tower with banded windows across the top (the second story was enclosed by a later owner). The wide, arched entryway shelters a handsome oak door, with a superb Arts and Crafts bronze cartouche. A unique feature of the interior of this house is that its floor plan was dictated by the client's insistence that none of the rooms contain four ninety-degree angles.

A couple of blocks south of the Eltse House, at 1962 Yosemite Road, Julia Morgan created a charming version of an English Country Cottage. The Wallace McGregor House was designed in 1920, and it uses its modest lot to maximum effect. This one-and-a-half-story stucco house has twin high-peaked gables, with banded latticed windows set into a wide dormer in the middle. There are smaller, angled dormers at both ends of the house, and the roofline on the south end slopes down over a sunroom with tall, latticed windows. The upstairs windows and dormers all have flower boxes underneath, and Morgan placed subtle, curved half-timber trim between the upper and lower windows on the front.

At the opposite end of Berkeley, near the Oakland border, Morgan designed a very unusual two-story stucco house with refined chalet-style detailing. The Dr. Arthur H. and Lily Wallace House at 2905 Piedmont Avenue was built in 1911. The low-angled gable has a wide bargeboard that is decorated with delicate Swiss folk-style carved patterns. A row of three paired casement windows across the upper story is underlined with a wide flower box. A large angled bay on the first story has latticed windows, with tracery in a Moorish pointed arch motif on the central window (a detail Morgan also used on the windows of the Walter Starr House in Piedmont, built the same year).

In the posh Claremont-Uplands neighborhood of Berkeley, in the shadow of the historic Claremont Hotel, Julia Morgan designed one of the most handsome Georgian Revival mansions in the Bay Area. The Elliot House at 1 Eucalyptus Road was designed in 1919 for a daughter of Elizabeth Glide. Its symmetrical two-and-a-half-story redbrick facade commands the crest of its raised lot, which is bordered by a brick retaining wall. The gambrel roof with five evenly spaced dormers, tall rectangular latticed windows, and deep pedimented portico sheltering an arched

ABOVE: William Colby House, Berkeley, 1905. BELOW: Professor Clifton Price Apartments, Berkeley, 1910.

dence is now used as student cooperative housing, but most of the rooms on the first floor remain as Morgan designed them.

A few blocks east of the UC campus, on a steep, narrow, winding road above Memorial Stadium, Julia Morgan created an elegant version of a Mediterranean villa. The Dr. W. L. Jepson House, at 11 Mosswood Road, was designed in 1929. It has large windows on its western facade to capture both the afternoon sunlight and the full bay view with its breathtaking sunsets. Concrete gateposts and a cast-iron gate guard the southeast corner of the level entry lot. Morgan used pastel stucco for the exterior of this two-story house, red clay tiles on the roof, and rounded arches on the first-floor windows. A delicate wrought-iron pattern of birds and acorn branches borders the front doorway. There are angled bays with banded windows at the corners of the second floor, and a massive brick chimney on the south end.

doorway with a neo-Palladian motif, give the Elliot House the appearance of a mid-eighteenth-century country estate on the Eastern seaboard.

A few blocks away, at 160 The Uplands, Julia created a superb, individualized version of a Tudor Revival–style residence for Mrs. Elizabeth A. Glide (another daughter of Elizabeth Glide) in 1916. The two-story home has a projecting central pavilion with half-timbering and a thick bargeboard on its peaked gable. The upper story of this pavilion has banded plateglass windows framed with heavy timbering, while the lower level forms an open porch supported by massive wood posts over the front entrance. Paired sets of banded plateglass windows flank the central pavilion, one on each story, and there is an overhang on the upper level. On the eastern end of the Glide House is a substantial sunroom with tall plateglass windows and a deck with half-timber walls on top.

Just east of the UC Berkeley campus, at 2833 Bancroft Steps, Morgan designed an impressive brick and stucco two-and-a-half-story residence with Prairie overtones. The Richard Clark House was built in 1913, where Bancroft Way becomes a pedestrian-only pathway. It nestles into a steep downslope lot, with the front facing south. Morgan used brick facing for the lower portion of the facade and stucco on the upper story. The Clark House has paired windows lined with flower boxes on the lower level, and a wide brick stairway and open porch leading to the front door. The second story has an overhang with a narrow wrought-iron balcony and three sets of banded windows. The horizontal lines and massing of the Clark House, together with its low-hipped roof, are elements of Frank Lloyd Wright's Prairie School of design. The resi-

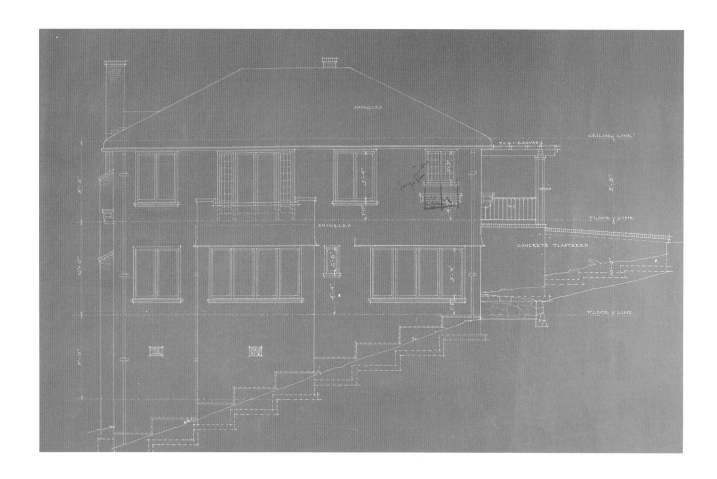

TOP: Mitchell-Williams House, Berkeley, 1915, south elevation. Courtesy of Jim Pfaffman and Katherine Pearson.
ABOVE: Mitchell-Williams House, Berkeley, 1915, east/west elevation. Courtesy of Jim Pfaffman and Katherine Pearson.

ABOVE: Mitchell-Williams House, Berkeley, 1915, living room, looking west.
RIGHT: Mitchell-Williams House, Berkeley, 1915, living room, looking south.

On Hawthorne Terrace, just below Euclid Avenue in the North Berkeley foothills, Morgan designed two superb, substantial houses that face each other but which are unalike in every other way. The Agnes Culver House at 1411 Hawthorne Terrace was designed in 1926, and is a fine example of a Spanish Colonial mansion. The rich salmon-pink stucco walls, red clay–tile roof, and ornate wrought-iron grillwork over the first-floor windows lend an air of authentic eighteenth-century Spanish craftsmanship to this two-story residence, as do the quoins at the corners and the elegant loggia around the entrance portico. The home is set well back from the street on a lushly landscaped lot, adding to the baronial ambience.

Across the street, at 1404 Hawthorne Terrace, Julia designed an Arts and Crafts–style masterpiece for Professor F. I. McCormac in 1911. This

LEFT: Dr. Arthur H. and Lily Wallace House, Berkeley, 1911. RIGHT: Ralph Eltse House, Berkeley, 1915.

three-story brown-shingle residence has low-angled gables facing west and south, with wide overhanging eaves. The third floor has banded latticed windows around both corners to take full advantage of the panoramic views of San Francisco Bay and the Berkeley Hills. A wide bay on the second story is lined with diamond-paned leaded windows, creating a magnificent sunroom effect with views in three directions. The entrance to the McCormac House is on the west, well off the street up a set of stairs, providing maximum privacy for the occupants.

One of the most magnificent Italian Renaissance Revival homes ever built in the East Bay is the one Julia Morgan did for Seldon and Elizabeth Glide Williams (another daughter of Elizabeth A. Glide), at 2821 Claremont Boulevard, in the Claremont Uplands area of Berkeley. Morgan designed this two-story palazzo-style residence in 1928. The

two-story symmetrical facade has a low-hipped roof with red clay tiles, pastel stucco walls, a wrought-iron balcony in the center of the second story, a heavy oak door with superb bas-relief coffered panels, and a colorful fresco pattern around the entryway. All the windows around the south side of the house have intricate Venetian Gothic tracery.

Upon entering the Seldon Williams House, visitors are often overwhelmed by the beauty, richness, and warmth this residence radiates. The soaring two-story entry hall is overlooked by the second-floor landing above, while straight ahead the tall picture-glass window has a wonderful pattern of Moorish tracery across the upper half. A lovely della Robbia of Madonna with Child, chosen by Julia Morgan, graces the top of the wall above this picture window, and the heating vents are disguised with intricate Moorish-style screens. To the right of the entry hall is the living room,

Professor F. I. McCormac House, Berkeley, 1911.

ABOVE: Richard Clark House, Berkeley, 1913. Courtesy of Lynn McMurray. BELOW: Richard Clark House, Berkeley, 1913, entry hall. Courtesy of Lynn McMurray.

which has an intricate redwood frieze lining the top of the walls and a marble-faced fireplace flanked with Venetian-style columns in concrete.

The most surprising room in this house, and the favorite of most visitors, is the sunroom at the south end. This open, light-filled space is lit by floor-to-ceiling banded plateglass windows that are framed by intricate Venetian Gothic tracery. These were some of the first sliding glass windows in California, engineered by Morgan so they could slide easily into wall pockets to the left or right. The polished marble floor in this sunroom has an unusual pattern of alternating dark and light tiles, and the furniture here is original to the house.

Adjacent to the sunroom, on the east end of the house, is a handsome library with Gothic arched niches of Australian gumwood in the middle of each wall between the rows of built-in bookshelves. The windows overlook the serenely landscaped backyard and have tracery that repeats the Gothic arched motif. To the north of the library is a charming breakfast room, with diamond-paned curved French doors framed by blue and yellow frescos in grapevine patterns. The view from this room is toward the guesthouse at the rear of the lot, with an adjoining wall adorned by Renaissance frescos done by Maxine Albro, famous for her murals in San Francisco's Coit Tower.

LEFT: Elliot House, Berkeley, 1919. BELOW: Mrs. Leslie Glide House, Berkeley, 1916. Courtesy of Lynn McMurray.

The largest and richest room in the Seldon Williams House is the formal dining room at the northwest corner. This long, elegant chamber is well lit by the tall, paired windows across the front. Morgan installed the same redwood frieze as in the living room, and the wide doorways are framed with splendid redwood paneling. This room was used by the vice chancellor of the University of California when his family resided here in the 1970s and '80s, and the guests who dined here included the governor of California. The house has since reverted to a private residence and has retained all of the grace and charm of Julia Morgan's original design.

Piedmont is a leafy, prosperous community in the hills above down-town Oakland. It was first settled in the 1850s as an unincorporated suburb and grew slowly until 1906, when the San Francisco earth-quake brought an influx of prominent families from across the bay. These were people who had spent pleasant summers in the Piedmont hills, and who now decided to build their new residences there. By 1907, the city had grown enough to be incorporated as a city. In the census of 1910, Piedmont had no

FACING, TOP: Dr. W. L. Jepson House, Berkeley, 1929. FACING, BOTTOM: Dr. W. L. Jepson House, Berkeley, 1929, front door detail. ABOVE: Agnes Culver House, Berkeley, 1926. LEFT: Agnes Culver House, Berkeley, 1926, detail of loggia.

fewer than thirty-two millionaires among its residents, giving it the largest per capita income of all communities of similar size in United States.[5] Since its founding, Piedmont has remained a strictly residential community, with almost no commercial or multi-unit development.

Julia Morgan designed nearly twenty homes in Piedmont between 1907 and 1930. These include some of her grandest residential designs, as well as modest bungalows that were built as speculative housing. At 11 Sierra Avenue, Morgan created one of her most refined essays in the Late Italian Renaissance mode. The Allen Chickering House was built in 1911. The facade of this two-story stucco house was inspired by the country villas of sixteenth-century Italian architect Andrea Palladio. It has a low-hipped roof and is completely symmetrical. The identical pavilions at each end have latticed windows on the second story, each with its own ornate wrought-iron balcony. The two-tiered, recessed central portico has superb neoclassical detailing, with Ionic pilasters, Tuscan columns, and an open pediment above the entrance. A brick footpath leads to a raised brick entry patio adorned with neoclassical urns.

LEFT: Seldon and Elizabeth Glide Williams House, Berkeley, 1928, detail of fresco around front doorway. BELOW: Seldon and Elizabeth Glide Williams House, Berkeley, 1928. FACING: Seldon and Elizabeth Glide Williams House, Berkeley, 1928, entry hall.

A few doors away, at 45 and 49 Sierra Avenue, Morgan built two spec houses for Addison Smith in 1907. Number 45 blends elements of both the California Bungalow and Prairie styles, with battered (upward sloping) walls sheathed in stucco, and a wide, flat front bay with banded arched windows. Number 49 is a one-and-a-half-story neo-Tudor house, with a high-peaked gable, half-timbering, a projecting bay with banded windows, and an arched brick entryway.

A few blocks east, further into the Piedmont hills, Julia Morgan created an unusual version of a Mediterranean villa with Spanish Colonial details. The Walter Starr House, at 216 Hampton Road, was designed in 1911 and built in 1912. The interior fit the needs of its original owners

ABOVE: Seldon and Elizabeth Glide Williams House, Berkeley, 1928, dining room.
LEFT: Seldon and Elizabeth Glide Williams House, Berkeley, 1928, view from the living room to the entry hall.

TOP: Seldon and Elizabeth Glide Williams House, Berkeley, 1928, sunroom. ABOVE: Seldon and Elizabeth Glide Williams House, Berkeley, 1928, detail of sunroom window. RIGHT: Seldon and Elizabeth Glide Williams House, Berkeley, 1928, breakfast room.

ABOVE: Ben Reed House, Piedmont, 1920. FACING: Allen Chickering House, Piedmont, 1911.

perfectly, with its warm redwood paneling, elegant fireplaces, handsome staircase, and French doors opening onto a lushly wooded lot. The exterior of the two-story Walter Starr residence is sheeted in pastel stucco, with an ornate wrought-iron balcony across the upper level on the north side, and Mission-style arched windows framed by columns on the first floor. The most intriguing detail is the delicate Moorish pointed-arch tracery that delineates the wide bay windows.

A few blocks down the hill, along Farragut Street, are three of Julia Morgan's finest Period Revival mansions. The Ben Reed House, at 200 Crocker Avenue at Farragut, is a superb Italian Renaissance Revival villa designed in 1920. It has an octagonal three-story entry pavilion, with a graceful esplanade (or curved double staircase) leading to the heavy oak front door. The portico has a curved pediment supported by Roman Order columns, and there are paired, diamond-paned casement windows set into the upper two stories of the entry pavilion. The most original feature of the Reed House is Morgan's use of an open redwood ceiling on the third floor of the pavilion, with beams that radiate outward from the center like spokes of a wheel, in a manner reminiscent of an eighteenth-century Shaker barn.

Walter Starr House, Piedmont, 1911, living room.

A block to the east, at 62 Farragut Avenue, is the mammoth Lombard House, a four-story Tudor Revival manor that rises like an Elizabethan great hall from its block-long lot. This is one of the largest private residences ever completed by Julia Morgan. It was designed in 1914 and built in 1915. The Lombard Mansion incorporates the normal complement of Tudor Revival details: high-peaked gables with bargeboards, an overhang on the third story, half-timbering, and lead-latticed windows. But Morgan's sophisticated handling of the sloping rooflines, pleasing fenestration, and rhythmic massing of the brick chimneys transcends the usual stylistic repertoire of other large Period Revival residences.

Across the street, at 246 Seaview Avenue, Richard R. Ayer commissioned Julia Morgan to design a two-story residence in 1913. The Ayer House was completed in 1914, and it reflects the cultural heritage of its

ABOVE: Walter Starr House, Piedmont, 1911, library. LEFT: Walter Starr House, Piedmont, 1911, main staircase.

ABOVE: Richard R. Ayer House, Piedmont, 1914, library (photo from c. 1915). Courtesy of Alan and Sara Hirsch. LEFT: Richard R. Ayer House, Piedmont, 1914, entry hall (photo from c. 1915). Courtesy of Alan and Sara Hirsch.

owner. Richard Ayer was of German ancestry, so Julia created a half-timbered, German Medieval-style house for him. There are two high-peaked gables in front, with bargeboards that have carved grape patterns. Below the central gable on the second story of the entry pavilion, Morgan placed a squared bay, with three lead-latticed windows. Below each of these windows are plaster panels, with superb bas-relief designs of grape clusters and vines surrounding a cartouche. The first floor is made of redbrick, as is the front porch. Across the top of the porch is a subtle Gothic arch of wood, decorated with an exquisitely carved pattern of grapes on the vine. The original entry hall, living room, dining room, library, and staircase in the Ayer House have remained almost intact.

One of the most distinctive residences Julia Morgan designed in the East Bay is the Charlotte Playter House, which was built for the Piedmont mayor's daughter in 1907. This stately two-and-a-half-story residence has a deceptively modest facade facing the street, at 612 Montain Avenue. The steeply pitched roofline slopes down over an unusual Gothic-arched porte cochere, with a wide triple-lighted dormer placed above it.

However, the west facade of the Playter House, which overlooks the spacious backyard, creates the impression of a country estate on the East Coast. Two low-sloping gables punctuate the hipped roof. Below the larger gable, on the left, are latticed and plateglass windows across the two upper floors, and a tall angled bay on the first floor. The smaller gable, in the center, has an angled bay with latticed windows on the second story, and a wide square bay with banded plateglass windows on the first story. Around the right side of the house, Morgan placed a row of arched latticed windows on the upper story, and a large picture window on the south end. The Playter House, with its rambling proportions and mix of traditional and modern elements, resembles the English Garden Homes of the noted Arts and Crafts architect Charles F. Voysey.

One of the first residences Julia Morgan designed in Oakland was for Mr. Fred C. Turner, the developer who built the Turner Shops on Piedmont Avenue (see chapter nine). The residence she created for him still stands at 255 Ridgeway Avenue, a few blocks west of Piedmont Avenue. It was designed in 1907 and completed in 1908. (Morgan added a one-car garage in 1915.) In addition to being a prominent developer, Turner became Oakland's Commissioner of Public Health and Safety.[6]

The Turner House is a classic example of a brown-shingle First Bay Tradition design, with its blend of historic and modern features and its use of natural materials to integrate into its spacious wooded lot. The entryway has a thick Moorish arch above the front door, large paired brackets on both sides, and a wide wooden awning overhanging the

TOP: Richard R. Ayer House, Piedmont, 1914. ABOVE: Richard R. Ayer House, Piedmont, 1914, detail of plaster decoration above front porch.

ABOVE: Lombard House, Piedmont, 1914. BELOW: Lombard House, Piedmont, 1914, east side.

doorway. The two-and-a-half-story house has a gabled roofline and banded casement windows, with leaded upper lights on the ground floor. The interior retains much of its original appearance, including three fireplaces and a grand balustraded staircase with diamond-paned, leaded windows above a wide landing. All of the main rooms have a spacious, elegant feeling, typical of Morgan's large residential designs.

At 400 – 34th Street, about three-and-a-half blocks above Telegraph Avenue in Oakland, Morgan designed a handsome Arts and Crafts house for Dr. Edward Von Adelung in 1909. This two-story brown-shingle residence originally stood at 407 – 29th Avenue. It was moved several years ago and converted into doctors' offices.[7] The Von Adelung House has a hipped roof and a wide balustraded balcony across the second story on the street side. There is a two-story entry pavilion on the east side, with banded, diamond-paned windows across the upper level and a rounded arch with a keystone above the front door. A triple-lighted bay to the left of the entrance and shelf molding above the first-floor windows are distinctive

Charlotte Playter House, Piedmont, 1907. Courtesy of Lynn McMurray.

George Walker House, Alameda, 1909.

touches. Three balconies on the east facade and three dormers above the entry pavilion were removed when the house was remodeled into offices.

About three miles north, at 6487 Benvenue Avenue, in Oakland's Rockridge area, Julia designed a solid two-story brown-shingle residence for Judge L. G. Harrier in 1908. The Harrier Residence has wide, over-hanging eaves with exposed roof beams and a wood awning that projects over the first story along the east facade. An unusual feature of this home was Morgan's use of shingled Doric columns to form a recessed entrance portico beneath the awning on the south facade. She also used three sets of paired Doric columns as a pergola on the east side of the house to create a trellis-shaded patio.

Alameda is an island city lying along the eastern shoreline of San Francisco Bay, separated from Oakland by a narrow estuary. By the early twentieth century, hundreds of upper-middle-class families had built their dream homes in an area along the southeastern edge of Alameda called the Gold Coast. Julia Morgan designed two of the most interesting homes in the Gold Coast, which have retained their original appearance and setting.

At 1232 Bay Street, Morgan created an impressive neo-Tudor Revival residence for George Walker in 1909. This two-and-a-half-story stucco-and-brick house has several classic Tudor features: twin high-peaked gables with bargeboards, hints of half-timbering on the upper levels, diamond-paned windows set into a small dormer, and a second-story overhang with

exposed beam ends. But the Walker House also has some atypical elements as well: a recessed entryway that opens onto the side of its spacious lot; a wide, double-gabled dormer facing the street; clinker brick lining the first story; and a covered balcony above the front entrance with fine metal grillwork.

A few blocks to the west, at 1025 Sherman Street, Morgan built an unusual version of a Prairie-style residence for Mrs. Alfred A. Durney in 1913. The Durney House is a two-story stucco home, with low-angled gables facing the front and side of the lot. The banded plateglass windows in the front gable have unique geometric trim around them. To the left of this gable is a recessed balcony, sheltered by the overhanging eaves above. Below the balcony is a long bay, with three picture-glass windows bordered by engaged Tuscan columns. A wide porte cochere extends off the right side of the house, and the elegant front entrance faces the driveway. With its horizontal massing, simple stucco surfaces, and use of banded windows, the Durney House is reminiscent of some of Frank Lloyd Wright's early residences in Oak Park, Illinois.

ABOVE: Fred C. Turner House, Oakland, 1907–8. RIGHT: Fred C. Turner House, Oakland, 1907–8, detail of east side.

TOP: Mrs. Alfred A. Durney House, Alameda, 1913. ABOVE, LEFT: Judge L. G. Harrier House, Oakland, 1908. Courtesy of Lynn McMurray. ABOVE, RIGHT: Dr. Edward Von Adelung House, Oakland, 1909. Courtesy of Lynn McMurray.

George W. Wilson House, Vallejo, 1907–9.

Vallejo is an old city along the northern shore of San Francisco Bay. In 1854, it was the site of one of the first United States naval bases on the West Coast. Although the Mare Island Naval base closed in 2001, during its heyday it lead to a steady influx of naval officers and other middle-class settlers to the residential district on the heights above the base. This area today is a city-designated historic zone called the Heritage District. Julia Morgan designed one of her most sophisticated homes in the First Bay Tradition within this Heritage District.

The George W. Wilson House, at 728 Capitol Street, was designed in 1907 and completed in 1909. For this commission, Morgan deftly blended elements of the Swiss Chalet style with neoclassical Beaux-Arts features. This two-and-a-half-story residence has a low-gabled roof with overhanging eaves and brown-shingled walls. The elegantly carved pattern on the bargeboard is typical of Morgan's use of fine wood craftsmanship. The front of the house is completely symmetrical, with banded windows below the gable, a wide balustraded balcony on the second floor, and a stately portico around the entrance. On the east side, Morgan placed a covered balcony above a large sunroom, with banded plateglass windows to catch the morning light. This is one of Morgan's finest residences in the First Bay Tradition mode.

Chico is a small historic city at the northern edge of Gold Rush Country. It is best known as the site of Chico State University. On the fringes of the university campus, at 341 Mansion Drive, Julia Morgan designed a graceful Mediterranean home for Dr. D. H. Moulton in 1921. The symmetrical two-story facade, with its red clay–tiled, low-hipped roof, round-arched latticed windows, and entry pavilion with a curved doorway, has an air of subtle beauty. Morgan placed recessed wings at each end of the house, with sunrooms on the second story that open out onto small balconies. The Moulton House was finished in 1923. It was later bought by the university and used as the President's Mansion from 1945 to 1993. It currently houses the Warren Reception Center.

Mr. and Mrs. Harry Gwin House, Petaluma, 1929.

Petaluma is a delightful small town in Sonoma County, about thirty-five miles north of San Francisco. It has an attractive historic district, which has been used as a location in several Hollywood movies ever since Alfred Hitchcock began filming in this area in the 1940s. The town had grown enough by the early twentieth century to attract a steady stream of middle-class professionals, who hired architects to build substantial homes. Four of the houses that Julia Morgan designed in Petaluma are excellent examples of her remarkable diversity.

At 14 Martha Street, on the edge of Petaluma's historic downtown, Morgan created a graceful Cape Cod, Georgian Revival residence for Mr. and Mrs. Harry Gwin in 1929. It commands its spacious, hilly lot, with views of most of southern Sonoma County. This two-story house has clapboard siding, latticed dormers set into its gabled roof, a recessed entry portico, and balconies along the second story with fine Chinese latticework patterns.

TOP: Dr. D. H. Moulton House, Chico, 1921–23. ABOVE: Dr. D. H. Moulton House, Chico, 1921–23, detail of entry.

J. Edgar Allen House, Petaluma, 1911.

A few blocks to the north, at 210 West Street, Morgan designed a perfect gem of an Italian Renaissance villa for Mr. A. Agius in 1934. The two-story Agius House has a hipped roof with red clay tiles and a symmetrical facade with stucco walls. Across the middle of the second story, Morgan inserted a balcony behind an elegant recessed loggia, with delicate arches and a fine wrought-iron railing.

About a mile south of Petaluma's old downtown are two more superb Julia Morgan residences. At 707 D Street, she designed a unique essay in the Prairie mode for J. Edgar Allen in 1911. The Allen House is one-and-a-half stories, with a stucco facade and half-timber trim between the first and second floors, and banded latticed windows around the west corner of the house. The most dramatic feature of this house is Morgan's use of a sweeping, low-angled roofline with wide, overhanging eaves, which she echoed on a smaller scale over the porte cochere on the east end.

Two blocks away, on a quiet, tree-lined cul-de-sac named Brown Court, Morgan designed a fine example of a New England Federal-style residence at number 15, for Mr. H. C. Scrutton in 1909. In classic Federal fashion, the Scrutton House displays a pleasingly symmetrical, rectangular facade, with whitewashed shakes along its walls, and latticed windows with green louvered shutters. The front entrance has a recessed doorway, with a fine curved pediment above it, and delicate leaded sidelights. Morgan remodeled the north wing of the residence in the 1920s, connecting it to a garage and servants' quarters.

ABOVE: Mr. A. Agius House, Petaluma, 1934. BELOW: H. C. Scrutton House, Petaluma, 1909. Photo by Peg King.

Twenty miles south, in the heart of tony Marin County, the verdant village of San Anselmo nestles at the base of the coastal range, in the shadow of Mount Tamalpais. The San Francisco Presbyterian Seminary occupies a beautiful sylvan campus along the east edge of the town. Julia Morgan designed two houses on the campus, the most impressive of which is the President's House, at 47 Seminary Road. The three-story brown-shingle residence is a skillful blending of the Arts and Crafts and Prairie styles. The main facade presents a long horizontal mass, with a low-angled roofline and minimal ornamentation. In the center is a large overhanging entry pavilion, supported by massive projecting brackets. This central pavilion has a neo-Palladian motif, with an arched central section and latticed sidelights. On each end of the second story are latticed casement windows.

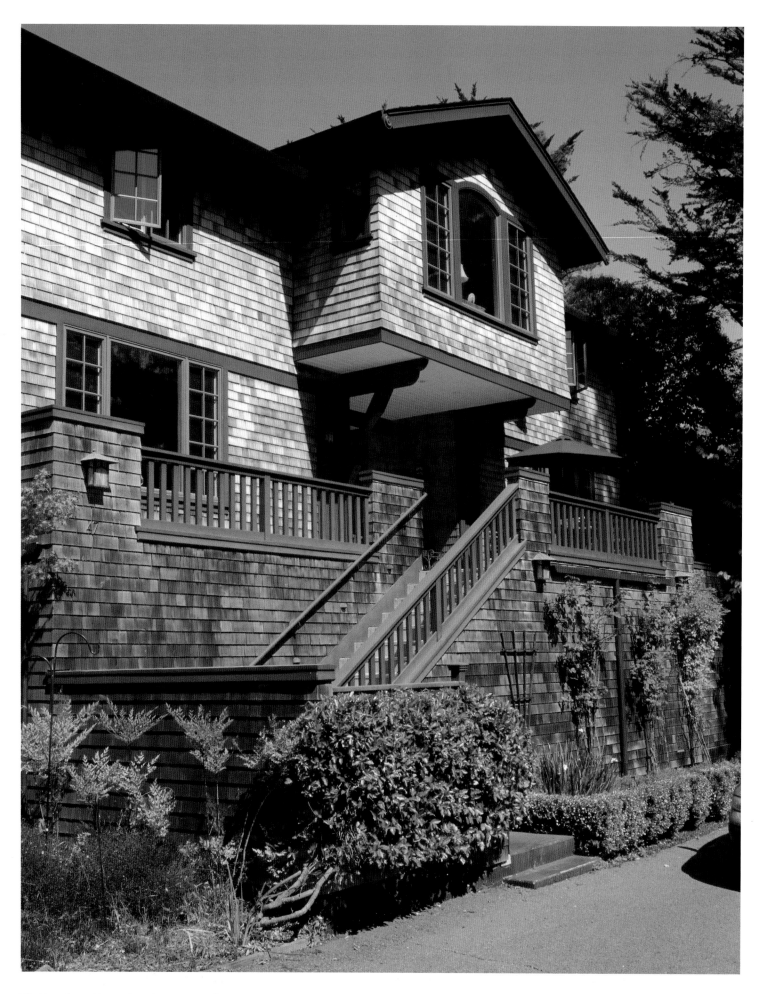

The President's House, San Francisco Presbyterian Seminary, 47 Seminary Road, San Anselmo, 1920–21.

Faculty House, San Francisco Presbyterian Theological Seminary, 118 Bolinas Avenue, San Anselmo, 1920–21. An Arts and Crafts–style residence with Prairie School overtones.

A few blocks to the west, secluded at the end of a leafy side street, is one of Julia Morgan's earliest individualized residences. The Bertha Newell House, at number 15 Prospect Street, was designed in 1907 and completed in 1908. It is a masterpiece in the Craftsman bungalow mode. The one-and-a-half-story home is set back well from the street, atop a hill at the rear of a large tree-shaded lot. The facade is sheathed with clapboards, and the wide overhanging eaves, low-angled gables, and deeply recessed corner porch with clinker brick facing are classic Craftsman bungalow features. Around the left corner is a sunporch with latticed windows, and on the right corner is a sunroom with banded casement windows. The interior of the Newell House is almost exactly as Morgan originally designed it.

Morgan designed another gem of a Craftsman bungalow in an exquisite setting, in the city of San Mateo, about ten miles south of San Francisco. The George Perry House, at 518 North Hurlingham Road, was built in 1912. Morgan placed the house near the back of a secluded lot, with a lovely garden in front. The low-angled roof slopes toward the street, and long, curved brackets frame the board-and-batten front door. Paired sets of latticed windows wrap around the right corner of the house, and half-timbering decorates the gable above. Morgan used elegant proportions on all the elements, giving the Perry House a rare sophistication for its modest size.

About fifteen miles south, in Palo Alto, Julia Morgan created a wonderful street-scale version of a Mediterranean villa for John

ABOVE: Bertha Newell House, living room, San Anselmo, 1907–8. FACING: Bertha Newell House, sunroom, San Anselmo, 1907–8.

George Perry House, San Mateo, 1912.

Kennedy in 1921. Located at 423 Chaucer Street, about one mile east of Stanford University, the Kennedy House sits close to the curb. Its symmetrical, two-story facade has a low clay-tile roof, white stucco walls, and a beveled, round-arched entryway. The most striking feature of this urban villa is the elegant floral pattern Morgan used on the wrought-iron grillwork across the central balcony, which she repeated on the rainspouts. The gabled chimney shows Maybeck's influence.

In Saratoga, one of the largest residences ever completed by Julia Morgan stands at the end of a quiet, winding cul-de-sac called Hayfield Court. The two-story, 13,000-square-foot Chauncey Goodrich House was designed in 1920, and has stucco walls with red-

wood trim. It has a magnificent setting, overlooking a spacious oval lawn, relandscaped by the current owner. The Goodrich residence is in the style of an English country estate, and is reminiscent of early-twentieth-century mansions on Long Island. The hipped roof slopes down over a sunroom on the south end, and a large, open porch on the north end. Twin gabled pavilions frame a central entryway, which is set beneath an overhang that runs across the entire facade, supported by massive wooden posts. Above this entrance is a triple-gabled dormer, underlined with decorated concrete flower boxes. The downstairs rooms in the Chauncey Goodrich House have retained most of their original architectural features.

BELOW: John Kennedy House, Palo Alto, 1921. RIGHT: John Kennedy House, Palo Alto, 1921, detail of wrought-iron grillwork on balcony.

ABOVE: Chauncey Goodrich House, Saratoga, 1920.
LEFT: Chauncey Goodrich House, Saratoga, 1920, library.

ABOVE: Chauncey Goodrich House, Saratoga, 1920, living room.
BELOW: James Pierce House, San Jose, 1908–10.

San Jose is one of America's ten largest cities, with about one million residents inside its city limits. However, it was still a small town in the early twentieth century, with a population of just fifty thousand in the 1910 census.[8] At that time, The Alameda was San Jose's most fashionable boulevard, lined with fancy residences in all the popular styles of the Edwardian era. At 1650 The Alameda, Julia Morgan created one of the most elegant mansions in San Jose, the James Pierce House. It was designed in 1908 for the vice president of the Pacific Manufacturing Company, the largest supplier of wood products on the West Coast.[9] The Pierce Mansion is a grand, two-story stucco residence, with a Prairie-style exterior and a neo-Georgian interior; an unusual blend of styles masterfully executed by Morgan.

The Pierce Mansion has the low-hipped roof with flat, overhanging eaves, banded windows, and clean horizontal lines and massing that are hallmarks of the Prairie style. On the right side is a marvelous porte cochere with volutes at each corner, and a sunroom above it. A handsome balustraded brick walkway leads to the massive front door, made of rare walnut burl. In the center of the facade is a double bay, with a squared bay above a gracefully curved one.

NORTH ELEVATION

WEST ELEVATION

TOP: James Pierce House, San Jose, 1908–10, front elevation. Courtesy of Robert Cullen. ABOVE: James Pierce House, San Jose, 1908–10, west elevation with porte cochere. Courtesy of Robert Cullen. FACING: James Pierce House, San Jose, 1908–10, detail of main staircase.

ABOVE, LEFT: James Pierce House, San Jose, 1908–10, detail of built-ins in dining room. ABOVE, RIGHT: James Pierce House, San Jose, 1908–10, detail of fireplace in living room. FACING: Mr. W. V. Dinsmore House, Pacific Grove, view from living room into dining room.

The common rooms on the first floor of the Pierce Mansion are all light, spacious, and elegant. The entry hall has a grand balustraded staircase made of walnut, and the front door and walls are paneled in walnut burl. The landing is lit by pairs of leaded windows on each side and framed by newel posts capped with stylized urn finials. The living room is huge, separated from the entry hall by pocket doors, and paneled in rich mahogany. The fireplace has a neoclassical mantel, with leaded-glass, built-in bookshelves on each side, and there are arched windows with delicate Art Nouveau patterns in the upper corners. To the left of the entry hall is a large projecting sunroom, with fan-lighted arched windows. The sunroom was enclosed years after the home was built, and is now used as an office. The adjacent dining room has wonderful

built-in china shelves, with leaded-glass doors that include a unique pattern of a California Mission bell tower. The Pierce Mansion was lovingly restored by its current owner and converted into office space.

In Pacific Grove, Julia Morgan designed a seaside residence that skillfully blends Craftsman and Prairie elements for Mr. W. V. Dinsmore in 1914. Overlooking Monterey Bay, at 104 – 1st Street, the Dinsmore House has low-sloping rooflines with overhanging eaves, horizontal massing, and banded picture windows around the side facing the ocean, which give it a Prairie feeling. The use of local natural materials, such as redwood shake siding and fieldstone steps, and the way the home seems to grow out of its natural setting, are classic Arts and Crafts features. The interior has marvelous Arts and Crafts details in all of the

downstairs rooms, with open-beamed ceilings, warm wood paneling, and exquisite patterns and colors on the wallpaper. The current owner has completed a painstaking restoration of these rooms.

Six miles to the south, in Carmel, stands one of the last residences designed by Julia Morgan, at 2981 Franciscan Way, overlooking the eighteenth-century Carmel Mission Church. This was a retirement cottage built in 1940 for Drs. Charles and Emma Pope. The single-story Pope Cottage presents a simple, utilitarian facade to the street, with its nearly flat roof, plain redwood walls, and floor-to-ceiling latticed windows along the front. The interior feels light and open, with bleached redwood paneling and an open-beamed ceiling. The most impressive feature of this home is the lovely view of the Mission and Carmel Valley, which Morgan framed perfectly in the living room bay window.

In Santa Barbara, in the tony Montecito district three miles east of downtown, Julia Morgan created a handsome Georgian Revival ballroom for

ABOVE: Mr. W. V. Dinsmore House, Pacific Grove, 1914. LEFT: Mr. W. V. Dinsmore House, Pacific Grove, living room.

Ferdinand and Gertrude Bain, for their estate "The Peppers," at 430 Hot Springs Road. Formally called the "Music Room," it was designed in 1915 and completed in 1917.[10] The ballroom Morgan designed for the Bains is magnificent, with nearly three thousand square feet of space and perfect acoustics. The ceiling has boxed beams, the walls are paneled with redwood wainscoting, and the floors are made of oak and mahogany. The tall, latticed windows and doors admit lots of sunlight. The baronial-scale fireplace was made from cast cement, and has ornate, neoclassical volutes and bas-relief figures on the mantelpiece.

Ojai is a quiet coastal community in Ventura County, about sixty miles north of Los Angeles. In this comfortable middle-class town, Morgan constructed her earliest Southern California residence, the F. B. Ginn House, in 1907. This rustic two-story home sits in the middle of a heavily wooded parcel, above Thatcher Street, east of McNell (it has no street address). The first floor of the Ginn House is made of warm fieldstone, as is the massive end chimney. The windows on the first level are deeply carved into the stone walls, and the corners taper slightly

ABOVE: F. B. Ginn House, Ojai, 1907. RIGHT: Ferdinand and Gertrude Bain House, Santa Barbara, "The Peppers," ballroom addition, 1915–17, detail of stairs. Photo by David Sullins.

inward. The second story is made of wood, with brown-shingle sheathing. Banded casement windows line the upper walls just below the low-gabled roof, which has wide, overhanging eaves with bargeboards and exposed beam ends. This is a superb First Bay Tradition home, perfectly integrated into its Southern California setting.

Beneath the leafy canopies of one of the oldest streets in Beverly Hills, in 1939, Julia Morgan did an extensive remodeling of a home for William Randolph Hearst and Marion Davies. The Hearst/Davies House at 1700 Lexington Road served as a residence for the couple when they were in the Los Angeles area. Morgan's remodeling work was so extensive that both the size and appearance of the existing house are her design.[11] The house sits in the middle of a sizeable parcel along a curved driveway, with tall brick pillars topped by urns flanking both entrances. The facade of this two-story, semi-

ABOVE: The Hearst/Davies House, Beverly Hills, 1939. LEFT: The Hearst/Davies House, Beverly Hills, 1939, detail of windows. FACING: Lily Yates House, San Francisco, 1911.

Elizabethan-style home has white stucco with half-timbering on the second floor, and whitewashed brick on the first floor. The low-hipped roof has flat clay tiles, and there are eight diamond-paned, banded windows above the front entrance, arranged in two rows of four. Morgan's most distinctive feature here is the gabled entry porch, which has heavy, curved brackets supporting overhanging eaves lined with scalloped bargeboards.

The most intriguing aspect of Julia Morgan's residential work in San Francisco is the wide variety of settings in which she designed homes for her clients in this City by the Bay. San Francisco is world famous for its many hills, and one of the steepest is the one that dominates the Russian Hill district. The 1100 block of Filbert Street has one of the steepest grades of any avenue in the city, and it was

here, at number 1126, that Morgan designed a three-story residence and rental unit for Mrs. Esther Woodland and Miss J. H. Caruthers in 1908. The views from this brown-shingle, three-story building are spectacular, overlooking Coit Tower and the bay, with the Berkeley Hills in the distance.

The Woodland and Caruthers House is a tall structure on a narrow lot, and it sits flush with the sidewalk. It has a Dutch Colonial gambrel roof with a pent eave. The top floor overhangs the second story and has banded latticed windows on the front and east side. The second story overhangs the first, with an angled bay in front, and the first floor has a wide squared bay. The building now sits above a brick-faced, four-car garage that was added when the current owners did a thorough restoration.

In a quiet residential neighborhood called Jordan Park, tucked between the Presidio and Golden Gate Park, Julia Morgan designed one of her most

ABOVE: Mrs. Esther Woodland and Miss J. H. Caruthers House, San Francisco, 1908–9.
FACING: Carriage house for Edwin and Jane Newhall Mansion, San Francisco, 1915.

subtly sophisticated Arts and Crafts homes for Lily Yates in 1911. Partially hidden from view behind large shade trees at 85 Jordan Avenue, the Yates House is a two-and-a-half-story stucco residence with Tudor Revival elements: high-peaked gables with bargeboards on the roof and all of the dormers, and an overhang on the second story. But the most distinctive feature of the home is Morgan's use of delicately refined leaded-glass patterns on the upper lights of the banded windows, which line the wide entrance pavilion. Angled bay windows below the main gable, and flower boxes below each dormer, add to the home's elegant ambience.

Presidio Heights is one of the toniest neighborhoods in Northern California. Historic mansions rise majestically above the quiet streets in this enclave of wealthy professionals, and there are stunning views of the Golden Gate and the North Bay from every intersection. On one of the poshest blocks in Presidio Heights, at 3630 Jackson Street, Julia Morgan created a superb Elizabethan-style manor house for Mr. Abraham Rosenburg in 1917. Rosenburg was known as "The Dried Fruit King of Fresno" before moving to San Francisco, and the residence Morgan designed for him is of truly baronial proportions.

The Rosenburg Mansion is a two-and-a-half-story home, with concrete walls and redwood beams. Unlike many of its neighbors, it has a side

entrance set back well from the sidewalk, down a brick path. The roof is covered in slate, and there is a high-peaked gable facing the street, with a five-light, lead-latticed bay below it. The entryway is sheltered by an L-shaped facade, with an overhanging bay that wraps around the second story. This bay has banded latticed windows, separated by paired Ionic pilasters. The glazed front door is framed by clustered columns, with a Tudor arch above. The entry hall remains as Morgan designed it, with a grand balustraded staircase and an open sight line through the dining room to a small garden off the street.

A few blocks east, at 2974 Pacific Avenue, in the equally affluent district of Pacific Heights, is one of Julia Morgan's most unusual commissions. Here, in 1915, she designed a garage and chauffeur's apartment for Edwin and Jane Newhall, who had built a huge Dutch Colonial mansion in the middle of the block.[12] This is a very simple, two-story, brick-faced structure that nonetheless displays some of Morgan's hallmark features: latticed casement windows with flower boxes beneath, and a symmetrical facade. The handsome appearance and solid construction of this small residence shows that Morgan put as much care into her residential designs for working people as she did with the homes of her wealthy clients.

Presidio Terrace is a gated community of impressive historic homes just south of the sylvan grounds of the former military base. The residents here have included many of the movers and shakers of San Francisco, including U.S. Senator Dianne Feinstein. At 36 Presidio Terrace, Julia Morgan designed a gorgeous Italian Renaissance Villa for Mrs. Elizabeth Watt in 1909. The Watt House was completed in 1911, and it has a two-story symmetrical facade, with a side entrance off the street at the end of a brick path. A lovely wrought-iron balcony graces the center of the second story. The horizontal roofline is adorned by bas-relief panels, with dynamic scrollwork patterns. Morgan placed elegant keystones above the second-story windows and the recessed front door, which is flanked by vaulted benches and neoclassical urns.

St. Francis Wood is one of the most beautiful residential districts in the United States, and one of the oldest planned communities in the nation. This is one of the few neighborhoods in San Francisco where all the streets are lined with trees and the houses have substantial yards. The meticulously maintained community west of Twin Peaks was planned in 1912, and most of the homes here were built before 1935.[13]

At 195 San Leandro Way and Monterey Street in St. Francis Wood, Julia Morgan designed a handsome version of a New England Georgian-style residence for Dixwell Davenport in 1916. This two-story brown-shingle

residence has a gabled roof, brick end chimneys, and a symmetrical facade. The tall, latticed windows have shelf molding above them along the first floor. There is a simple arched entryway, with a recessed front door framed by delicate sidelights and a transom.

Two blocks to the north, at 67 San Leandro Way, Morgan designed a particularly refined Tudor Revival residence for Reverend Robert Donaldson in 1921. The Donaldson House was completed in 1922, and it has high-peaked gables and pastel stucco walls. The most distinguishing feature of this two-story home is Morgan's sophisticated fenestration; a wide, projecting bay below the front gable has five banded, diamond-paned windows, and there are arched, lead-latticed windows on the first floor. The entrance is on the side, and the massive oak front door has panels carved with curtain-molding patterns.

ABOVE: Mr. Abraham Rosenburg House, San Francisco, grand staircase. LEFT: Mr. Abraham Rosenburg House, San Francisco. FACING: Abraham Rosenburg House, San Francisco, 1917.

ABOVE: Reverend Robert Donaldson House, San Francisco, interior window detail. LEFT: Reverend Robert Donaldson House, San Francisco, exterior window detail. FACING: Mrs. Elizabeth Watt House, San Francisco, 1909–11.

The Sea Cliff area is one of the most visually dramatic neighborhoods on the West Coast. Tucked away into the northwest corner of San Francisco, between the Presidio and Lincoln Park, this small enclave of elegant homes offers breathtaking views of the Golden Gate Bridge and the Marin Headlands. Here, at 50 Scenic Way, Julia Morgan designed a modest Mediterranean-style home for Maude B. Strobridge in 1922.[14] The Strobridge House makes maximum use of its narrow lot, with its north-south room orientation and the entrance on the west side. This is a two-story stucco residence, with a low-gabled roof clad in red clay tiles, and arched fanlight windows on the first level of the west and south sides. The south side presents a symmetrical facade to the street, with banded latticed

widows graced by a wrought-iron balcony on the second floor. The only ornament Morgan used on the exterior of the house was a pair of swags that flank the balcony, and a cartouche above the arched doorway. The interior was remodeled and enlarged in the 1980s, but Morgan's original plan of framing a gorgeous view of the Golden Gate Bridge with picture windows on the north side of the house has been retained.

Just across the Golden Gate, in the small Marin County town of Belvedere, a little south of Tiburon, Julia Morgan designed an impressive Italian Renaissance–style mansion for Gordon Blanding in 1913. This substantial two-story home stands at 450 Belvedere Road, and is part of an estate that includes an earlier house by Willis Polk. The Blanding

Mansion was nicknamed "The Casino" after Morgan's design was completed in 1914. It has three dormers set into a low-hipped roof, round arched windows, a delicate wrought-iron balcony across the front, and a deeply recessed loggia on the second story. Morgan sited the Blanding residence so it faces San Francisco Bay, in order to take full advantage of the superb panoramic views.

TOP: Dixwell Davenport House, San Francisco, 1916. ABOVE: Gordan Blanding House, Belvedere, 1913. Courtesy of Lynn McMurray. FACING: Maude B. Strobridge House, San Francisco, 1922.

CHAPTER 12

An Enduring Legacy

"Her buildings really have a timeless quality; she created structures in which people continually experience a sense of well-being, even a century or so after they were built."

—Kit Ratcliff, architect

Julia Morgan closed her office at the Merchants Exchange Building in 1950, after more than forty-two years of active practice as an independent architect. During the last several years of her life, she became almost a recluse due to failing health, and had only a handful of visitors to her San Francisco apartment. One of her few outings during this period, a trip to Oakland to visit old haunts, ended in her being mugged and severely injured. After that, her secretary, Lilian Forney, hired live-in nurses to attend to her needs, as both her strength and her memory rapidly diminished. She died on February 2, 1957, at the age of eighty-five.

For many years after her death, Julia Morgan was almost a forgotten figure. The rise of the Late Modern movement in architecture, which had begun before the end of her career, gained momentum as such styles as Bauhaus International and Concrete Brutalism displaced the Beaux-Arts and other decorative styles during the 1950s and '60s. The work of architects like Morgan and Maybeck was considered by critics and architecture schools to be "derivative" at best, and "false" at worst.

One of the few exceptions to the general dismissal of Julia Morgan's work after her death was Bay Area architecture critic Allen Temko. He was almost alone in his positive assessment of her career when he wrote the following indignant response to a September 1957 *Life Magazine* article about Hearst Castle, which didn't even mention Julia Morgan. "In American architecture, she deserves at least as high a place as does Mary

Cassatt in American painting, or Edith Wharton in American letters."[1]

As recently as the early 1980s, many critics were still dismissing Julia Morgan's body of work as unoriginal and uninspired. The respected architectural historians David Gebhard and Robert Winter, for example, wrote disparagingly about her abilities in *A Guide to Architecture in Los Angeles and Southern California* (1982). In the entry on Hearst Castle, of which they wrote, "viewed as a whole, it is a disappointment," these authors concluded with this snide assessment of Morgan's skills as an architect:

But like most of Julia Morgan's work, the architecture is dry, and exhibits little in the way of sensitive handling of overall forms and details. The client can be blamed for the continual changes and growth of the project, but he cannot be blamed for the insensitive rendering of the architecture.[2]

With the advent of the postmodern movement in the late 1970s and early 1980s, architects began to reintroduce a variety of colors, materials, and forms in their work, and incorporate historic motifs into their designs. As the public taste in architecture began to shift away from the soulless, sterile ambience of glass-and-steel boxes and concrete slabs toward a more humanistic and nature-based aesthetic, critics, academics, and historians began to reassess Julia Morgan's legacy and praise her for her sensitivity to clients' needs and her creativity, versatility, and adaptability in a wide variety of settings. Such books as *Building with Nature*,

FACING: Grace Dodge Chapel/Auditorium, Asilomar, 1915, view of the stage. ABOVE: Julia Morgan in 1926 at age fifty-four, during the height of her career.

ABOVE: Window detail, Seldon Williams House, Berkeley, 1928. FACING: The Roman Pool at Hearst Castle, 1930–35.

by Leslie Freudenheim and Elizabeth Sussman (1974), *Bay Area Houses*, by John Beach and Sally Woodbridge (1976), and *Julia Morgan: Architect*, by Sarah Boutelle (1988), helped to inform their readers about Julia Morgan's considerable contributions to American architecture and increase awareness of her unique role in the history of the profession.

Today, those successful architects who are familiar with Julia Morgan's career and body of work have a very high opinion of her skills as a designer, and her legacy. One such architect is Kit Ratcliff, president of The Ratcliff Architects, located in Emeryville, across the bay from San

Francisco. The firm was founded in 1906 by Kit's grandfather, Walter Ratcliff Sr., who had an illustrious career designing distinguished homes in the Bay Area for more than forty years. Walter Ratcliff Sr. was an acquaintance of Julia Morgan's, and Kit grew up knowing Walter Steilberg, Morgan's former draftsman. The Ratcliff Architects have a well-respected practice, with about fifty-five architects and designers. Their focus is on institutional designs, such as academic, civic, and health-care facilities, but they also have done several adaptive reuse projects for historic structures. Roughly half of their current design staff is made up of women.

Kit Ratcliff is quite effusive in his assessment of Julia Morgan's place in American architecture. "She's a little like Florence Nightingale. Here's a woman who was very active in a profession that was dominated by men, and who had an uphill battle the whole time to establish her credibility in an old-boy environment." He went on to mention that "twenty or thirty years ago, women architects in our office who went to a construction site would be given less than their due, or even ridiculed by some of the construction crew. Today, I can't imagine that happening, and Julia Morgan's pioneering efforts absolutely had a lot to do with this change in attitude toward women in our profession."

In assessing Julia Morgan's body of work, Kit Ratcliff emphasized what he calls the "durability" of her buildings as their most outstanding quality. "She had integrity in her use of materials, which leads to durable architecture. Her buildings all possess those three attributes that Vitruvius said were essential to good architecture: commodity, fitness, and delight. In other words, they perform a necessary function, their design fits the needs of that function, and they delight the senses."

"When you go through one of her buildings," Ratcliff went on to say, "one can see how they possess these attributes. Her buildings really have a timeless quality; she created architecture in which people continually experience a sense of well-being, even a century or so after they were built. People want to preserve her buildings because they can keep using them, and adapting them to their current needs. And people want to preserve both the exterior and interior of her buildings as much as possible, because of their high quality of workmanship, and the integral nature of her whole designs."

Cynthia Ripley has been working as an urban designer and architect in Northern California for nearly forty years. She received her M.A. in architecture from UC Berkeley in 1969. She started her own design firm in 1980, and her husband became a partner in the firm in 2003. Ripley-Scott Architects is located in Napa, California, and their practice is

focused on civic and academic projects, with some residential work. Since 1980, the staff has ranged between ten and twenty architects and draftsmen, and the design crew has often been 50 percent female.

"There were only three or four female owners of architecture practices when I started my firm in 1980," Cynthia recalls. "When I went to school at UC Berkeley, Julia Morgan was in the air as one of the architects who was active in the First Bay Tradition. I was always determined not to be strictly a residential architect, and I was impressed by Julia Morgan's ability to work in varied scales, and with a wide range of styles and materials—which is what I wanted to do."

"I've always been amazed at how prolific she was," Cynthia continued, "especially since she did it all on her own—without a husband or father to support her. But then, of course, there aren't many individual patrons like Phoebe Hearst anymore. Morgan also had the ability to work at the site, discussing design issues with builders and craftsmen in the field—which is a skill that is not that common in our profession today."

"But what I like most about Julia Morgan," Cynthia Ripley summed up, "was that she didn't make a big deal about being a woman architect. She just was a total professional about her work, and did her job well. That's why she was accepted and respected in an all-male field as the only independent woman architect at that time."

At UC Berkeley's Environmental Design Department, Julia Morgan's body of work is featured in many of the architectural history courses students are required to take to earn an M.A. in architecture. Professor Kathleen James-Chakraborty has taught architectural history at Berkeley for more than fourteen years. Her area of expertise is twentieth-century American architecture, and she discusses Julia Morgan's career in both the general survey and twentieth-century classes she teaches.

"I always describe Julia Morgan when I talk about the Beaux-Arts style, as well as some of the more eclectic, woodsy buildings that were part of the Bay Area movement in the early twentieth century," Kathleen explains. "I also discuss her early use of more modern building materials, especially concrete. And I point out to my students local examples of her work with these modern materials, such as the Berkeley Women's City Club and the Hearst Memorial Gymnasium on campus. We take students on a walking tour of campus architecture, and include both the Hearst Gymnasium and Girton Hall. I regularly have students in my survey course choose to write a research paper about one of her buildings, because they've become interested in her career."

"What strikes me as noteworthy about Julia Morgan's work," Kathleen continues, "is the high level of craftsmanship, and a degree of understatement in her more woodsy designs. They deliberately don't draw attention to themselves, but are more subtle and blend in with their environment more than the work of many other architects of her time. But above all else, she is an inspiration to women in the profession, to know that a woman ran a practice that large that long ago. She was off the national radar screen for many years after she died. But then with the rediscovery of her work that began in the late 1970s, she became an inspiration for many young women architects around the country."

A new generation of architects and designers, entering the field during the past decade, has also been influenced by Julia Morgan's legacy. Mirren Fischer is an architect with the firm of Cambridge Seven Associates, in Cambridge, Massachusetts. She has been practicing architecture in the Boston area since 2000, and worked as an interior designer in San Francisco for two years before that. Ms. Fischer was raised in the W. L. Jepson House at 11 Mosswood Road, designed by Julia Morgan in 1929 (see chapter eleven). She remembers during her childhood being surrounded by beautiful homes in her neighborhood just above the UC Berkeley campus. But it was Julia Morgan's design of the residence she grew up in that left a special impression on her.

When asked if growing up in such a house had influenced her decision to become an architect, Mirren responded affirmatively. "I'm sure it must have had some influence, as the house is superbly sited and scaled, and the circulation and detailing are beautifully done. I can't help comparing most modern housing, where each house so often looks like all the others, with the grace and proportion of Julia Morgan's designs."

Some young professionals in the high-tech industry have been inspired to change their careers to architecture after studying Julia Morgan's career. Kristina Feliciano had worked as a quality documentation supervisor at a biotech firm in South San Francisco for six years when she decided to start taking architectural history courses and learn more about the interesting older buildings she had grown up with in the Bay Area. In 2006, she decided to apply to several of the nation's top architecture programs, in order to train for a new career as an urban designer.

"My field of architecture will be sustainable design, and I was definitely inspired to go into this field after studying Julia Morgan's work," Kristina explained. "I've noticed that Julia Morgan's buildings have lasted because they have evolved and have been put to use by later generations. Many of her buildings have been put to new uses that have equal or greater value to society than their first use, yet they retain their original qualities of beauty and exquisiteness, because of her attention to detail and dedication to excellence in all her designs. The modern practice of sustainable design in architecture really echoes the main principles of the First Bay Tradition, with its emphasis on using local, natural materials, and integrating into the environment."

"Another thing that has inspired me about Julia Morgan's work," Kristina added, "is that even when she was designing servants' quarters, like at the Seldon Williams House in Berkeley, she applied her principles of attention to detail and careful design. So when Julia Morgan designed a wealthy client's residence, even the servants could all live in an environment of beauty."

No single book can capture the scope of a career as brilliant and prolific as Julia Morgan's. Yet within these pages, I hope readers have gained some understanding of her remarkable achievements, both as a pioneer for women in her field and as an innovative and sensitive designer of all types of human spaces. When I began writing this book, I considered myself an expert on Julia Morgan's work. However, during the process of researching and describing roughly 20 percent of her completed buildings, I have gained far greater respect and admiration for what she achieved in so short a period of time.

Frank Lloyd Wright had a career that stretched across sixty-six years, from 1893, when he opened his own practice, until his death in 1959. In that time, he completed a total of about 532 buildings, according to the records of the Frank Lloyd Wright Foundation.[3] Thus, Frank Lloyd Wright produced an average of eight buildings per year. Julia Morgan's independent design career lasted forty-two years, from 1904, when she opened her own office, until 1946, when she finished her last new designs. During that time, she completed a total of nearly 750 commissions (including structures such as piers and aqueducts). Thus, Julia Morgan produced an average of about eighteen structures per year, more than twice Frank Lloyd Wright's output. And as my fellow researcher Lynn McMurray points out, people are still discovering more buildings that Julia Morgan designed, a process which undoubtedly will continue for many years to come.

Far more important than the amazing quantity of Julia Morgan's buildings is their exceptional quality and extraordinary variety. The photos and drawings in this book bear witness to the uncommon beauty of Julia Morgan's designs. But they are a poor substitute for the real thing. So I urge readers who want to truly understand Julia Morgan's unique legacy to experience her work for themselves by exploring as many of her buildings as they can. It will be a delightful and inspirational journey, and one which will leave you grateful for the life and career of this talented woman who wouldn't take no for an answer.

Window detail, Chapel of the Chimes, Oakland, 1928.

Notes

Introduction:

1. According to the Encyclopedia Britannica, the first woman to have an architecture office in the United States was Louise Blanchard Bethune, who opened an office in Buffalo, New York in October, 1881, in partnership with her fiancé Robert Bethune, whom she married that December. She did not have a license, and she learned architecture as a draftsman in the firm of Waite and Caulkings. The first licensed woman architect in America was Sophia Hayden, who was admitted to the architecture program at MIT in 1886, and graduated in 1890. After designing the Woman's Building at the 1893 Chicago World's Fair, she gave up the idea of practicing architecture and became active in women's societies. Thus, it seems safe to say that Julia Morgan became the first licensed, independent woman architect in America when she opened her own office in San Francisco in 1904 without a partner.

Chapter 1:

1. Interview with Lynn McMurray, Antioch, California, October 2005.

2. Interview with Lynn McMurray, Antioch, California, October 2005.

3. Photo Archives, Julia Morgan Collection, Cal Poly, Robert E. Kennedy Library.

4. Interview with Lynn McMurray, Martinez, California, November 2005.

5. Sara Boutelle, *Julia Morgan, Architect*, New York, Abbeville Press, 1988, 25.

6. Student Enrollment Records, (1868–1952), Office of the Registrar, UC Berkeley.

7. Frank Carothers, Research Librarian, Engineering Library, UC Berkeley.

8. Boutelle, *Julia Morgan, Architect*, 23.

9. Berkeley Architectural Heritage Association (BAHA), Historic Resources Inventory.

10. Boutelle, *Julia Morgan, Architect*, 29–30.

11. Exhibit notes, "Architectural Drawings by Julia Morgan," Oakland Museum, January, 1976. In a letter from Julia Morgan to Aurelia Reinhardt, President of Mills College, dated September 10, 1917, she wrote that she almost went home without trying to gain admission to the Beaux-Arts after she found out that women were not even allowed to take the exam, ". . . when, unexpectedly, the French Government decided to admit women sculptors and painters . . . They did not say anything about the Department of Architecture, either way, it not entering their heads that there might be women applicants. So, I was given the benefit of the doubt, and allowed a chance with the other competitors . . ." Mills College archives.

12. Interview with Lynn McMurray, Martinez, California, May 2006.

13. Letter from Julia Morgan to Phoebe Hearst, February 16, 1899, George and Phoebe Apperson Hearst Papers, Bancroft Library, UC Berkeley.

14. UC Berkeley, College of Environmental Design, Julia Morgan Collection.

15. PBS documentary, *Julia Morgan: A Life by Design*, 1990.

16. California Architects Board, Sacramento, Board Minutes, April 1904.

Chapter 2:

1. Temko, Allan, "The Flowering of San Francisco," *Horizon*, January 1959, 9–10.

2. Copy of original building permit, on file at BAHA.

Chapter 3:

1. Julia Morgan's office records.

2. Olmsted, Roger, and T. H. Watkins, *Here Today; San Francisco's Architectural Heritage*, San Francisco, Chronicle Books, 1968, 81.

3. Julia Morgan's office records.

4. Interview with Marian Simpson, Julia Morgan Collection, Bancroft Library, UC Berkeley.

5. Talk by Walter Steilberg to Historical Guide Association of California, August, 1969, Regional Oral History Office, Bancroft Library, UC Berkeley.

6. Interview with Donald Mooers, Piedmont, California, July 1977.

7. Interview with Maynard P. Buehler, Orinda, California, June 2001.

8. Interview with Lynn McMurray, Martinez, California, January 2006.

9. Armstrong, Jane, "The Woman Architect Who Helped Build the Fairmont Hotel," *Architect and Engineer of California*, vol. 10, no. 3, October 1907, 69–71.

10. Ibid.

11. Walter Steilberg, unpublished article, 1969, Julia Morgan Collection, Bancroft Library, UC Berkeley.

Chapter 4:

1. "Women in Politics," *San Francisco Chronicle*, November 7, 2006, A10.

2. Historic Resources Inventory, BAHA.

3. Spain, Daphne, *How Women Saved the City*, St. Paul, University of Minnesota Press, 2001, 89.

4. Ibid., 90.

5. Julia Morgan's office records.

6. Interview with Ruth Hearn, Executive Assistant to the CEO of the YWCA, Los Angeles County, July 2006.

7. Ibid.

8. Ibid.

9. Sue Lee, Chinese Historical Society of America, San Francisco, California.

10. Riess, Suzanne B., "The Julia Morgan Architectural History Project," Bancroft Library, Regional Oral History Project, UC Berkeley, 1976, 138.

11. Carruth, Gorton, *American Facts and Dates*, New York, Harper Collins, 1993, 362–64.

12. "Historic Structures Report," Berkeley City Club, Carey and Company, Inc., October 30, 2005, 3.

13. Ibid., 6.

14. Julia Morgan's office records.

15. Interview with Lynn McMurray, Martinez, California, October 2006.

Chapter 5:

1. "Julia Morgan's Architecture," Asilomar State Beach and Conference Grounds.

2. Ibid.

3. "The Yosemite," John Muir, 1912, reprinted in *Asilomar Visitor's Guide,* no. 9, 2.

4. Al Hittle, Maintenance Director, Asilomar.

5. Ibid.

Chapter 6:

1. "Mills College; Mission and History," www.mills.edu/about/mission_and_history.php.

2. Karen Fiene, Campus Architect, Mills College.

3. Ibid.

4. Ann Clarke, Head of Schools, Julia Morgan School for Girls, July 2006.

5. Michelle Holmes, Vice President, American Baptist Seminary of the West, Berkeley.

6. Craig, Robert M., *Bernard Maybeck at Principia College*, Salt Lake City, Gibbs Smith, Publisher, 2004, 228.

Chapter 7:

1. Meads, Phillip F., Jr., "Julia Morgan and the First Baptist Church of Oakland," January 30, 2005 (unpublished article).

2. Ibid.

3. Historic Resources Inventory, BAHA.

Chapter 8:

1. Hillard, Richard, and Angele Lewis, "Chapel of the Chimes," copyright by Chapel of the Chimes, 1999.

2. Bunny Ghilardi, Administrative Assistant, Chapel of the Chimes.

3. Peterson, Dan, and Geraldine Peterson, *Santa Rosa's Architectural Heritage*, Sonoma County Historical Society, 1983, 12.

4. UC Berkeley, College of Environmental Design, Julia Morgan Collection.

Chapter 9:

1. Corbett, Michael R., *Splendid Survivors; San Francisco's Downtown Architectural Heritage*, San Francisco, Living Books, 1979, 85.

2. Kuzuri Jackson, Deputy Director, Potrero Hill Neighborhood House.

3. Native Daughters of the Golden West, www.ndgw.org., "About Our Order."

4. NDGW, Docent Handbook, March 1993, 6.

5. Statistical Abstract of the United States for 1920, Government Printing Office, Washington, D.C., 1921, 53.

6. Interview with Patti Taylor, President of the Monday Club, August 2006.

7. Ibid.

8. Statistical Abstract of the United States for 1920, 53.

Chapter 10:

1. "Hearst San Simeon State Historical Monument," California Sate Parks, 2001.

2. Interview with Walter Steilberg, Kennedy Library, Cal Poly, 56–57.

3. Letter from Hearst to Morgan, December 31, 1919, Kennedy Library, Cal Poly.

4. California State Parks, ibid.

5. Telegram from Morgan to Hearst, December 31, 1919, Kennedy Library, Cal Poly.

6. Hoyt Fields, Director, Hearst Castle State Historical Monument, November 2006.

7. Interview with Lynn McMurray, Martinez, California, November 2006.

8. Boutelle, *Julia Morgan, Architect*, 180.

9. Kastner, Victoria, *Hearst Castle: Biography of a Country House*, New York, Abrams, 2000, 32.

10. Carol Paden to author, March 1984.

11. Letter from Morgan to Hearst, January 1, 1922, Kennedy Library, Cal Poly.

12. Kastner, *Hearst Castle: Biography of a Country House*, 44–45.

13. Raveill, Ken, *Hearst Castle; A Pictorial Tour Guide*, Kansas City, Missouri, Terrell Creative, 2000, 30–44.

14. Dan Eller, Public Relations Specialist, California Department of Parks and Recreation, June 2006.

15. Kastner, *Hearst Castle: Biography of a Country House*, 179.

16. Letter to Bertha Forney from H. C. Forney, Valuation Engineer for Hearst Castle, October 14, 1935, collection of Lynn McMurray.

17. Dan Eller, June 2006.

18. Kastner, *Hearst Castle: Biography of a Country House*, 82–83.

19. Kastner, *Hearst Castle: Biography of a Country House*, 134.

20. Raveill, *Hearst Castle: A Pictorial Tour Guide*, 10.

21. Dan Eller, June 2006.

22. Panama-Pacific Exposition, Official Guidebook, 1915.

23. Dan Eller, June 2006.

24. Kastner, *Hearst Castle: Biography of a Country House*, 147.

25. Lynn McMurray to the author, October 2006.

26. Ibid., November 2006.

27. Ibid.

28. Ibid.

29. College of Environmental Design, UC Berkeley, Julia Morgan Collection.

Chapter 11:

1. Julia Morgan's Office Records.

2. Historic Resources Inventory, BAHA.

3. Edwards Transcripts, BAHA files.

4. Unpublished article by Betty Marvin, Historic Resources Inventory file, BAHA.

5. June Rutledge, President of Piedmont Historical Society, to author, September 1978.

6. Carter, Suzanne Howard, National Register of Historic Places Registration Form, May 2000, section 8, 16.

7. Lynn McMurray to author, November 2006.

8. Statistical Abstract of the United States for 1940, 1941, 26.

9. Gottschalk, Mary, "Julia-Morgan-designed Rose Garden Mansion Gets Overdue Restoration," Rose Garden Resident, September 21, 2006, 10–11.

10. Unpublished report by Christine Palmer, Palmer Historical Consulting, Santa Barbara, February 2003.

11. Job Records, Julia Morgan Collection, Kennedy Library, Cal Poly.

12. San Francisco Architectural Heritage files.

13. California Historical Society, San Francisco, files on St. Francis Wood.

14. Edwards Abstracts, San Francisco Heritage files.

Chapter 12:

1. Scharlach, Bernice, "Julia Morgan's Legacy," *California Living Magazine, San Francisco Chronicle*, August 24, 1975, 24.

2. Gebhard, David, and Robert Winter, *Architecture in Los Angeles and Southern California*, Salt Lake City, Peregrine Smith, 1982, 598.

3. Frank Lloyd Wright Foundation Web site: www.franklloydwrightfoundation.org.

Bibliography

BOOKS

Boutelle, Sara Holmes. Julia Morgan, Architect. New York: Abbeville Press, 1988.

Caldwell, Kenneth H. *Maybeck: Artisan, Architect, Artist*. Santa Barbara: Peregrine Smith, 1977.

Craig, Robert M. *Bernard Maybeck at Principia College*. Layton, UT: Gibbs Smith, Publisher, 2004.

Corbett, Michael R. *Splendid Survivors: San Francisco's Downtown Architectural Heritage*. San Francisco: Chronicle Books, 1978.

Freudenheim, Leslie M. *Building With Nature: Inspiration for the Arts and Crafts Home*. Layton, UT: Gibbs Smith, Publisher, 2005.

Gebhard, David, et al. *Guide to Architecture in San Francisco and Northern California*. Santa Barbara: Perigrine Smith, 1973, revised 1976.

Gebhard, David, and Robert Winter. *Architecture in Los Angeles and Southern California*. Layton, UT: Peregrine Smith, 1982.

Kastner, Victoria. *Hearst Castle; Biography of a Country House*. New York: Abrams, 2000.

Keeler, Charles. *The Simple Home*. Santa Barbara: Peregrine Smith, 1979 (re-issue of 1904 edition).

Longstreth, Richard. *On the Edge of the World: Four Architects in San Francisco at the Turn of the Century*. New York: Architectural History Foundation, Cambridge, Mass., and London, MIT Press, 1983.

———. *Julia Morgan, Architect*. Berkeley: Berkeley Architectural Heritage Association, 1984.

Marvin, Betty. *The Residential Work in Berkeley of Five Women Architects*. Berkeley: Berkeley Architectural Association, 1984.

Olmsted, Roger, and T. H. Watkins. *San Francisco's Architectural Heritage*. San Francisco: Chronicle Books, 1968.

Peterson, Dan, and Geraldine Peterson. *Santa Rosa's Architectural Heritage*. Santa Rosa, CA: Sonoma County Historical Society, 1983.

Quacchia, Russell L. *Julia Morgan, Architect, and the Creation of the Asilomar Conference Grounds*. Philadelphia: Xlibris Corporation, 2005.

Raveill, Ken. *Hearst Castle: A Pictorial Tour Guide*. Kansas City, MO: Aramark, 2000.

Spain, Daphne. *How Women Saved the City*. St. Paul: University of Minnesota Press, 2001.

Wadsworth, Ginger. *Julia Morgan, Architect of Dreams*. Minneapolis: Lerner, 1990.

Wilson, Mark A. *A Living Legacy: Historic Architecture of the East Bay*. San Francisco: Lexicos, 1987.

Woodbridge, Sally B., et al. *Bay Area Houses*. New York: Oxford University Press, 1976.

ARTICLES

Boutelle, Sara Holmes. "A Woman of Many Firsts." *Art*, Oakland Museum Association, January/February, 1976.

Gottschalk, Mary. "Julia Morgan–designed Rose Garden Mansion Gets Overdue Restoration." *Rose Garden Resident*, September 21, 2006, 1, 10–11.

Olson, Lynne. "A Tycoon's Home was his Petite Architect's Castle." *Smithsonian*, December 1985, 60–71.

Temko, Allan. "The Flowering of San Francisco." *Horizon*, January 1959, 4–23.

Scharlach, Bernice. "The Legacy of Julia Morgan." *California Living, San Francisco Chronicle*, August 24, 1975, 24–27, 29–31.

Wilson, Mark A. "The Maybeck Legacy." The Museum of California, November/December 1983, 14–15.

———. "Julia Morgan; Bestower of Beauty." *The Museum of California*, July/August 1984, 7–11.

Index

"WIRE CUT A GRAY"

T.C. SILLS

← CONTINUE   "STANDARD GRAY"

← "RUSTIC" GRAY

"STANDARD GRAY"

CEMENT

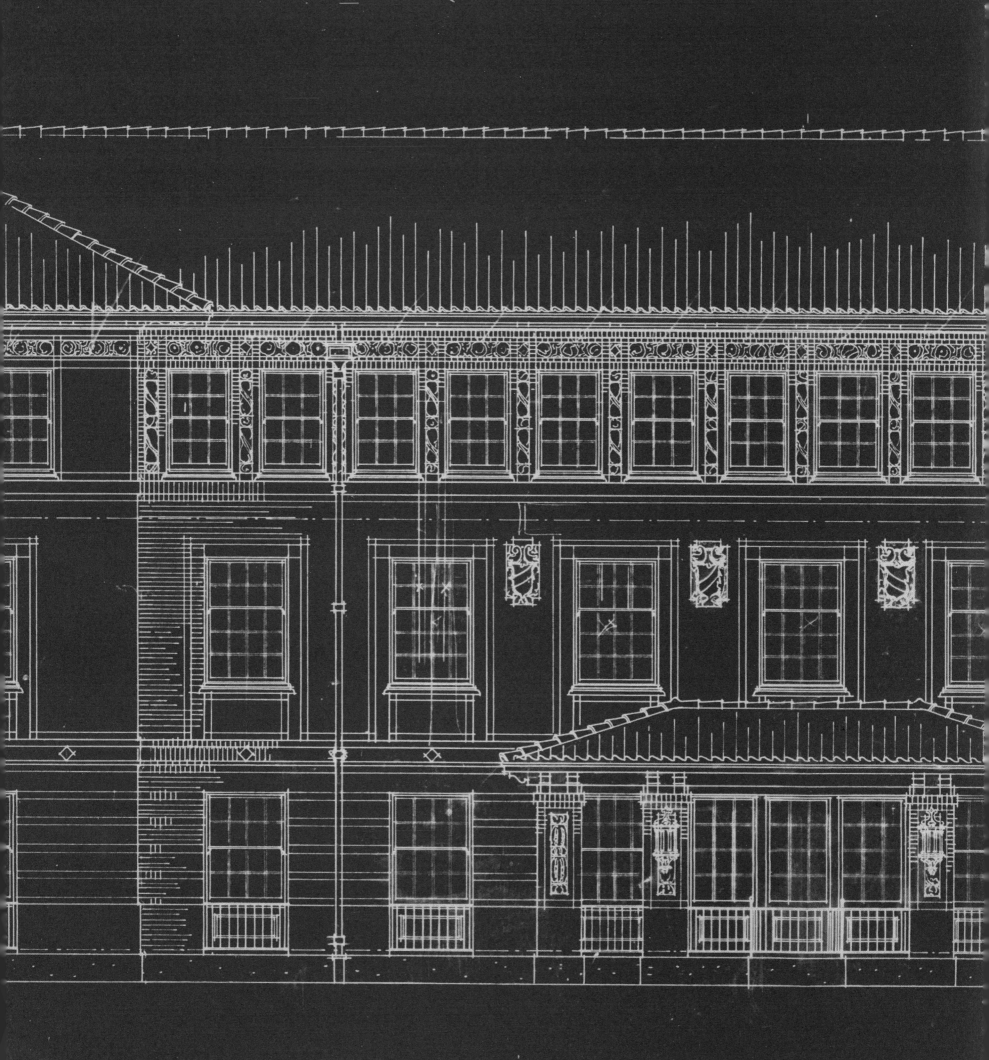